ESSENCE OF THE HEART SUTRA

THE PUBLISHER gratefully acknowledges Richard Gere and the Gere Foundation for helping to make the publication of this book possible.

ESSENCE OF THE
HEART SUTRA

THE DALAI LAMA'S
HEART OF WISDOM TEACHINGS

TENZIN GYATSO
THE FOURTEENTH DALAI LAMA

Wisdom Publications • Boston

Wisdom Publications
199 Elm Street
Somerville MA 02144 USA

ISBN-13: 978-0-86171-284-7

Cover design by Rick Snizik.
Interior design: Gopa&Ted2, Inc. Set in Centaur MT 12/17.

Printed in the United States of America.

Contents

Editor's Preface

The short Buddhist scripture entitled the *Heart of Wisdom*, the basis of His Holiness the Dalai Lama's teachings presented in this book, is one of the most sacred texts of Mahayana Buddhism, the Buddhism that traditionally flourished in India, China, Tibet, Japan, Korea, Mongolia, Vietnam, and many regions of central Asia, including what is today modern Afghanistan. For more than two millennia this scripture has played an extremely important role in the religious lives of millions of Buddhists. It has been memorized, chanted, studied, and meditated upon by those aspiring to attain what Mahayana Buddhism describes as the perfection of wisdom. Even today, the chanting of this sutra can be heard in Tibetan monasteries, where it is recited in the characteristically deep overtone voice, in Japanese Zen temples, where the chanting is done in tune with rhythmic beating of a drum, and in Chinese and the Vietnamese temples, where it is sung in melodious tunes.

Often referred to by its short title, the *Heart Sutra*, the interpretation of the subtle meaning of the various passages of this sacred text has produced numerous commentarial treatises over the centuries. In His Holiness' discourse, we are brought face to face with the rich history of textual interpretation that exists in a great spiritual tradition like Buddhism. So richly textured is the Dalai Lama's discourse presented here that this book effectively serves as a comprehensive introduction to the central teachings of Mahayana Buddhism.

Historically, the *Heart of Wisdom* belongs to a well-known class of Buddhist scriptures known as the Perfection of Wisdom sutras, which the noted European scholar Edward Conze, who dedicated much of his life in translating these scriptures, has suggested was composed some time between 100 B.C.E. to 600 C.E.[1] On the surface, these scriptures deal with the topic of the perfection of wisdom, which articulates the deep insight into what Buddhists call emptiness. However, as can be seen from both the Dalai Lama's discourse on the text and from the fifteenth-century Tibetan commentary provided in the appendix, there is a further, "hidden" level of meaning to the text that pertains to the progressive stages of spiritual development eventually culminating in the attainment of full enlightenment. Furthermore, these commentaries also demonstrate how the altruistic intention to attain buddhahood for the benefit of all beings, which is the fundamental motive behind a Mahayana Buddhist's spiritual quest, is deeply embedded in the meaning of the *Heart Sutra*. In other words, the central theme of these Perfection of Wisdom sutras is found to be a profound union of compassion and wisdom.

Perhaps to a reader unfamiliar with the Mahayana tradition, it may seem perplexing that a text such as the *Heart Sutra*, whose core message is a string of negative statements, can be a source of such deep spiritual inspiration to so many people. To dissolve this perplexity it is necessary to have some understanding of the role the language of negation plays in these Buddhist scriptures. From its earliest evolution, one of the central teachings of Buddhism has been to gain freedom from our bondage to clinging, especially to a belief in some kind of enduring reality, whether it be the external world or the internal world of one's own personal existence. According to Buddhism, the source of our suffering lies in a deeply embedded tendency to grasp at enduring realities where there are none, particularly the tendency to grasp at an enduring sense of self. It is this grasping that gives rise to dysfunction in our interaction with our fellow beings and with the world around us. Since this tendency is deeply rooted in the psyche, nothing short of a radical deconstruction of our naïve understanding of self and world can lead us to true spiritual freedom. The *Heart Sutra's* categorical negation of the intrinsic existence of all things, especially the five personal aggregates, can be seen not only as an extension of this key Buddhist wisdom but in fact as a supreme example of such wisdom. This is the key to the overwhelming veneration of this short text in the Mahayana Buddhist world.

In addition to being utilized for deep meditative contemplation on emptiness, the sutra is often chanted as a means of overcoming various factors that obstruct spiritual progress. For example, it is customary in the Tibetan tradition to recite the sutra at the beginning of every teaching session. I remember with fondness the palpable sense of anticipation I used to feel as a teenager when the *Heart Sutra* was recited at the large congregation of monks and lay people attending the Dalai Lama's teachings in Dharamsala, India in the early 1970s. The recitation concludes with the statement "May all obstacles be averted; may they be no more; may they be pacified," which is recited while clapping three times. The idea is that much of what we perceive as obstacles actually stem from the deeply ingrained clinging to our own existence and to the self-centeredness this produces. By reflecting deeply upon the essentially empty nature of all things, we undercut any basis for the so-called obstacles to take root within us. Thus meditation on emptiness, undertaken often on the basis of reciting the *Heart Sutra*, is considered a powerful method for overcoming obstacles.[2]

Today, I am deeply honored to serve as the translator for His Holiness the Dalai Lama's authoritative discourse on this sacred Buddhist text. I feel that, in my humble role as the Dalai Lama's translator, I have been given a precious opportunity to be part of a noble initiative to help enable others, especially millions of fellow Buddhists worldwide, to appreciate the deep insights embodied in this short sacred text.

There are many others whose role has been critical for the success of this project. First and foremost, I would like to express my deep admiration to His Holiness the Dalai Lama for always being such a great exemplar of the essence of the Buddha's teaching. I thank the Foundation for the Preservation of Mahayana Tradition (FPMT), especially its Spiritual Director, Ven. Zopa Rinpoche and his center, Land of Medicine Buddha, for organizing His Holiness' teachings in Mountain View, California, the transcripts of which form the primary basis of this book. Supplemental material came from a talk on the *Heart Sutra* given by His Holiness in 1998 sponsored by Three Rivers Dharma in Pittsburgh, Pennsylvania. I thank Patrick Lambelet for his initial editing, Gene Smith for locating the Tibetan text of Jamyang Galo's commentary, and David Kittelstrom and Josh Bartok, editors at Wisdom Publications, whose help has been invaluable in making the English text of this book clear and readable. Whatever merits there might be in this endeavor, may they help alleviate the suffering of all beings; may they help us humans to create a more peaceful world.

Thupten Jinpa, Montreal, 2002

Part I
Buddhism in Context

CHAPTER 1

The Quest for Inner Development

TIME IS ALWAYS moving forward. With each passing moment, beginning from the instant of our birth, we come closer to the end, to our death. That is our nature, and the nature of the universe. As spiritually minded people, it is essential for us to constantly check and examine ourselves, to see how we are living every moment of our lives. In my own case, the major portion of my life is already gone. But, although I am a lazy practitioner of Buddhism, I can see that each year there is some progress in my life. Above all, I try to be a genuine follower of Buddha Shakyamuni and a good Buddhist monk. Of course, even Buddhist monks make mistakes in our lives and practices, but I think I have made some contribution to this world we share, especially to the preservation of Tibetan Buddhist culture.

In spiritual matters, we should not allow ourselves to be too easily content, because truly there is no limit to our spiritual potential. All of us—any of us—can develop infinitely; and any of us can attain buddhahood. The mind we possess right now, though it may presently be full of ignorance and suffering, can eventually become the mind of an enlightened being, of a buddha. Where our material possessions are concerned, finding contentment makes sense. But since there is no limit to our spiritual potential and there is a limit to the span of our life, we must make every effort to utilize what little time we have as well as we possibly can with this precious human lifetime.

In being human, we are all the same. On that level, none of us are strangers. There are no fundamental differences between any of us. You experience many emotions; some emotions help you, others hinder you. The same is true for me. Within our ever-changing experiences, all of us are constantly experiencing different emotions— sometimes anger, sometimes jealousy, sometimes love, sometimes fear. You experience many thoughts; you have the potential to analyze, to investigate the long-term and short-term prospects for your life. The same is true of me. Within our ever-changing experiences, we all constantly experience different perceptions—color, odor, taste, feel, sound, even awareness itself. These things function similarly in each of us.

Of course it is also possible to find differences among human beings. We each have individual experiences not shared by everyone. For instance, you may have great skill with computers, while I have none. Likewise, since I have no mathematical training, I may have great difficulty with certain things that come quite easily to you. But these kinds of differences in individual experience are minor. You and I may hold different beliefs—about the universe, about reality, about religion. And even within a belief, within a faith tradition, for instance, there are all sorts of differences between people. But such differences in belief, just like differences in experience, are minor compared to our common humanity. The essential thing is that we are all the same in being human—thinking, feeling, and being aware. We all share this one planet, and we are all members of one big human family.

And I think too that some human experiences are universal. For instance, when someone smiles at you, you feel happy. In the exact same way, I feel happy when you smile at me. Both you and I seek out what we think is good for us, and we avoid what we think will harm us. This is basic human nature.

In the realm of the external material world, we are aware of what is good for us and what harms us. Then, on the basis of this careful analysis and clear knowledge, we try to create a joyful life, a successful life, the happy life that we all know is our birthright. Similarly, in the vast realm of our thoughts and emotions, we need careful analysis to develop clear awareness of what is harmful and what is helpful. So we must work to increase the positive elements of our minds and weaken the force of the negative elements. The positive elements enhance our happiness; the negative elements undermine it. Thus, a clear understanding of our inner world is of the utmost importance.

Since happiness cannot be achieved through material conditions alone, we need other means by which we can fulfill our aspirations. All the world religions offer means for fulfilling these aspirations, but I also believe that such means can be developed independent of any religion or any belief. What is required is recognizing the immense potential we have as human beings and learning to utilize it. In fact, today, even in modern science, there is a growing recognition of the relationship between the body and the mind and an emerging understanding of how our mental attitudes impact our physical health and well-being.

One very important faculty that we human beings have at our disposal to help find happiness and overcome suffering is our intelligence. Our intelligence can help us overcome suffering and find happiness, but our intelligence can also cause problems. Using our intelligence, we build homes and grow food, but through our intelligence we also create anxiety and fear. Our intelligence gives us the ability to remember the past, and it allows us to envision possibilities for the future—both good ones and bad. We cannot truly overcome unhappiness by physical comfort alone; ultimately, the unhappiness created by human intelligence can only be alleviated by intelligence itself. Therefore, using our intelligence appropriately is essential.

To do this, we must conjoin our intelligence to a warm, open heart. We must bring to our rationality a sense of compassion, of caring for one another, of sharing. These mental qualities transform our intelligence into a powerful positive force. The mind becomes broader and more spacious, and even when unfortunate incidents happen, the effect on our composure is minimal. We are able to care about the well-being of others and not just ourselves. In fact, as human beings, we are by nature social animals, and our happiness and even survival depend upon our interaction and cooperation. So when positive emotions guide intelligence, it become constructive. The warm, compassionate heart is the basis for peace of mind, without which the mind will always be uncomfortable and disturbed.

Anger and hatred, they destroy our inner peace. Compassion, forgiveness, a sense of brotherhood and sisterhood, contentment, self-discipline, these are the basis of peace—both external peace and inner mental peace. Only through strengthening these inner good qualities can a genuine, lasting peace develop. This is what I mean by spiritual development. I sometimes also describe this as inner disarmament. In fact, in all levels of our existence—family life, social life, working life, and political life—inner disarmament is, above all, what humanity needs.

CHAPTER 2

Religion in Today's World

MANY TEACHINGS, MANY PATHS

FINDING TRUE FULFILLMENT does not depend on following any particular religion or holding any particular belief. Many people do, however, look for fulfillment within religious practice or faith. When we remain isolated from one another we sometimes get distorted pictures of traditions or beliefs other than the ones we ourselves happen to uphold; in other words, we may mistakenly believe our own religion is somehow the only valid one. In fact, before I left Tibet and had close contact with other religions and other religious leaders, I myself held such views! But ultimately, I have come to see that all traditions have great potential and can play a very important role in benefiting humanity. All the world religions contain tools to address our basic aspiration to overcome suffering and increase happiness. In this chapter, we'll examine these tools.

Some religions have sophisticated philosophical analyses; some have extensive ethical teachings; some place a greater emphasis on faith. If we observe the teachings of the world's major faith traditions, however, we can discern two main dimensions of religion. One is what could be called the metaphysical or philosophical dimension, which explains why we are the way we are and why certain religious practices are prescribed. The second dimension pertains to the practice of morality or ethical discipline. One could say that the ethical teachings of a faith tradition are the conclusions supported and validated by the process of the metaphysical or philosophical thinking. Although the world's religions differ widely in terms of metaphysics and philosophy, the conclusions these differing philosophies arrive at—that is, their ethical teachings—show a high degree of convergence. In this sense, we can say that regardless of whatever metaphysical explanations religious traditions employ, they all reach similar conclusions. In some form or other, the philosophies of all world religions emphasize love, compassion, tolerance, forgiveness, and the importance of self-discipline. Through interfaith and interpersonal communication, sharing, and respect, we can learn to appreciate the valuable qualities taught by all religions, and the ways in which all religions can benefit humanity.

Within each path, we can find people who are truly dedicated to the welfare of others out of a deep sense of compassion and love. Over the past few decades, I've met quite a number of people from many different traditions—Christians, Hindus, Muslims, and Jews. And within every tradition, one finds wonderful, warmhearted, sensible people—people like Mother Teresa, who completely dedicated her life to the well-being of the poorest of the world's poor, and Dr. Martin Luther King, Jr., who dedicated his life to the peaceful struggle for equality. Clearly, all traditions have the power to bring out the best in human potential. Yet different traditions use different approaches.

Now, we may ask, "Why is this so? Why is there such metaphysical and philosophical diversity among the world's religions?" Such diversity can be found not only among different religions but also *within* religions as well. Even within Buddhism—even within the teachings of Buddha Shakyamuni himself—there is a great diversity of teachings. In Buddha's more philosophical teachings, we find this diversity to be most pronounced; in some cases, the teachings seem even to contradict each other!

This points, I think, to one of the most important truths about spiritual teachings: spiritual teachings must be appropriate to the individual being taught. The Buddha recognized among his followers a diversity of mental dispositions, spiritual inclinations, and interests, and saw that in order to suit this diversity he had to teach differently in different contexts. No matter how powerful a particular teaching may be or how "correct" a philosophical view may be, if it is not suitable to the individual hearing it, it has no value. A skillful spiritual teacher will thus judge the appropriateness of a given teaching for a given individual and teach accordingly.

We can draw an analogy to the use of medicine. Antibiotics, for instance, are immensely powerful; they are immensely valuable in treating a wide variety of diseases—but they are useless in treating a broken leg. A broken leg must be properly set in a cast. Furthermore, even in cases where antibiotics are indeed the appropriate treatment, if a doctor were to give an infant the same amount of medicine as she would a fully grown man, the child might well die!

In the same way, we can see that the Buddha himself—because he recognized the diversity of mental dispositions, interests, and mental capabilities of his followers—gave diverse teachings. Looking at all the world's religions in this light, I feel a deep conviction that all of the traditions are beneficial, each of them uniquely serving the needs of their followers.

Let's look at the similarities another way. Not all religions posit the existence of God, of a creator; but those that do emphasize that the devout should love God with all their heart. How might we determine whether someone loves God sincerely? Surely, we would examine that person's behavior and attitude toward fellow human beings, toward the rest of God's creation. If someone shows genuine love and compassion toward fellow human brothers and sisters, and toward the Earth itself, then I think we can be sure that that person truly demonstrates love for God. It's clear that when someone really respects God's message, they emulate God's love for humanity. Conversely, I believe that the faith of someone someone who professes belief in God and yet shows no love or compassion toward other human beings is highly questionable. When we look in these ways, we see that genuine faith in God is a powerful way to develop the positive human qualities of love and compassion.

Let's look at another differing aspect of world religions: belief in a previous life or a next life. Not all religions assert the existence of these things. Some, like Christianity, acknowledge a next life, perhaps in heaven or in hell, but not a previous one. According to the Christian view, this life, the present life right now, has been created directly by God. I can well imagine that if we really believe this sincerely, it would grant a feeling of deep intimacy with God. Surely, being aware that our very lives are God's creation, we would develop a profound reverence for God and the wish to live our lives thoroughly in accord with God's intentions, thereby actualizing our highest human potential.

Other religions or people may emphasize that we are each responsible for everything we create in our lives. This kind of faith can also be very effective in helping actualize our potential for goodness, for it requires that individuals take total responsibility for their lives, with all the consequences resting on their own shoulders. People who genuinely think in this way will become more disciplined, and take on full responsibility for practicing compassion and love. So while the approach is different, the result is more or less the same.

Maintaining One's Own Tradition

When I reflect in this way, my admiration for the world's great spiritual traditions increases, and I can deeply appreciate their value. It's clear that these religions have served the spiritual needs of millions of people in the past, continue to do so at present, and will continue to do so in the future. Realizing this, I encourage people to maintain their spiritual tradition, even if they choose to learn from others, like Buddhism, as well. Changing one's religion is a serious matter, and it should not be taken lightly. Given that different religious traditions evolved in accordance with specific historical, cultural, and social contexts, a particular tradition may be more suitable to a particular person in a particular environment. Only the individual knows which religion is most suitable for him or her. It is therefore vital not to proselytize, propagating only one's own religion, asserting that it alone is the best one or the right one.

Because of this, when I give Buddhist teachings to Western people of different religious backgrounds, I usually feel a little apprehensive. It's not my wish to propagate Buddhism. At the same time, it is quite natural that out of millions of people, some may feel that the Buddhist approach is more suitable for them, more effective for them. And even if an individual feeling this way gets to the point where he or she is considering adopting the Buddha's teachings, it is still very important to examine those teachings and that decision carefully. Only after thinking very deeply, examining very thoroughly, can one really determine that the Buddhist approach is, in one's own case, more suitable and effective.

Nonetheless, I think it's better to have some kind of faith, some kind of deeper belief, than none at all. I firmly believe that someone who thinks only of this life and only of worldly gain simply cannot attain lasting satisfaction. That kind of purely materialistic approach will not bring lasting happiness. When young and both physically and mentally fit, an individual might feel completely self-sufficient, completely in control, and thus conclude that no deeper faith or deeper understanding is necessary. But with time, things inevitably change; people get sick, grow old, die. These inevitabilities, or perhaps some unexpected tragedy that money can't fix, may clearly point out the limitation of this worldly view. In those cases, a spiritual approach, such as the Buddhist one, may become more suitable.

SHARING EACH OTHER'S TRADITIONS

In this diverse world, with its varied religious traditions, it's enormously valuable for practitioners of different religions to cultivate a genuine respect for each other's tradition based on dialogue. At the beginning of such a dialogue, it's important that all the participants fully recognize not only the many areas of convergence between each other's faith traditions, but more crucially, that they recognize and respect the differences between the traditions. Furthermore, we should look at the specific causes and conditions that gave rise to the different faith traditions—the historical, cultural, sociological, even personal, factors that affect a religion's evolution. In a sense, these things help us see *why* a particular religion came into being. Then, having clarified the differences and the origins, we look at the religions from a different perspective: becoming aware of how differing religious philosophies and practices can give rise to similar results. By entering into interfaith dialogue in this way, we develop genuine respect and admiration for each other's religious traditions.

There are, in fact, two kinds of interfaith dialogues: ones that take place on a fairly academic level, primarily concerned with intellectual differences and similarities, and ones that occur between genuine practitioners of different traditions. In my own experience, this latter type of dialogue has been of especially great help in deepening my own appreciation of other traditions.

Interfaith dialogue is just one of several ways that we can share in each other's traditions. We might also do this by making pilgrimages, journeying to sacred places of different traditions—and, if possible, praying or practicing together, or engaging in communal silent meditation. Whenever I have the opportunity, I pay my respects as a pilgrim at the holy places of different traditions. In this spirit, I have gone to the temples of Jerusalem, to the Lourdes sanctuary in France, and to various holy places in India.

Many religions espouse world peace and global harmony. Consequently, another means through which we can appreciate each other's religions is by seeing religious leaders come together and hearing them express this same value from the same speaking platform.

Bishop Desmond Tutu of South Africa pointed out to me an additional way through which we can share in each other's religious strength: wherever there is a disaster or some great tragedy in the world, people from different traditions can join together to help the people suffering, thereby showing the heart of each religion in action. I think this is a great idea, and furthermore, on a practical level, it is a wonderful opportunity for people of different traditions to get to know one another. I promised Bishop Tutu that in future discussions of interfaith sharing I would mention this idea—and now I am fulfilling my promise to him!

Thus there are grounds for promoting dialogue and harmony between religions, and there are methods. Establishing and maintaining this harmony is vitally important because without it people can become alienated from one another quite easily. In the worst case, conflict and hostility arise, leading to bloodshed and even war. Often some kind of religious difference or religious intolerance is at the root of many such conflicts. And yet, religion is supposed to cool hostility down, to ease conflict and bring peace. It is tragic when religion itself becomes just another basis for creating strife. When this happens, then religion has no value to humanity—in fact, it is harmful. Yet I don't believe we should do away with religion; religion can still be a basis for developing peace among the people of the world.

Furthermore, although we can point to great advances in technology, even in what we might call "quality of life," we still have certain difficulties that technology and money cannot solve: we feel anxiety, fear, anger, sadness at loss or separation. In addition to this, we have many day-to-day complaints—I certainly do, and I imagine you do as well.

These are certain fundamental aspects of simply being human that have remained unchanged for thousands, perhaps even millions, of years. These things are only overcome through peace of mind. And, in some form or other, all religions deal with this. So even in the twenty-first century, the various religious traditions still have a very important role—to provide us peace of mind.

We need religion in order to develop both this inner peace and peace among the world's peoples; that is the essential role of religion today. And in pursuit of this goal, harmony among the different traditions becomes essential.

LEARNING FROM OTHER TRADITIONS

Though I don't recommend that a person abandon his or her native religion, I believe that a follower of one tradition can certainly incorporate into his or her own spiritual practice certain methods for spiritual transformation found in other traditions. For example, some of my Christian friends, while remaining deeply committed to their own tradition, incorporate ancient Indian methods for cultivating single-pointedness of mind through meditative concentration. They also borrow some tools from Buddhism for training the mind through meditation, visualizations related to developing compassion, and practices that aid with increasing patience. These devout Christians, while remaining deeply committed to their own spiritual tradition, embrace aspects and methods from other teachings. This, I think, is beneficial to them and wise.

This borrowing can function the other way around as well. Buddhists can incorporate elements of the Christian tradition into their practice—for instance, the tradition of community service. In the Christian tradition, monks and nuns have a long history of social work, particularly in the fields of health and education. In providing service to the greater human community through social work, Buddhism lags far behind Christianity. In fact, one of my German friends, himself a Buddhist, told me of his observation that over the past forty years, although many large Tibetan monasteries have been built in Nepal, very few hospitals or schools have been built by the monasteries. He remarked that if these monasteries were Christian, then along with an increase in the number of monasteries, there would surely have been an increase in the number of schools and healthcare facilities as well. A Buddhist can express nothing in response to such a statement other than full agreement.

Buddhists can certainly learn a great deal from Christian service. On the other hand, some among my Christian friends express a deep interest in the Buddhist philosophy of emptiness. To these Christian brothers and sisters, I have observed that the teaching of emptiness—the teaching that all things are devoid of any absolute, independent existence—is unique to Buddhism, and therefore perhaps a deeply committed Christian practitioner might be wise not to delve too deeply into this aspect of Buddhist teaching. The reason for this caution is that if someone begins to delve deeply into the Buddhist teaching of emptiness and truly pursues it, it can undermine one's faith in a creator—an absolute, independent, eternal being that is, in short, not empty.

Many people profess deep reverence for both Buddhism and Christianity, and specifically for the teachings of Buddha Shakyamuni and Jesus Christ. Without a doubt, it's of great value to develop profound respect for the teachers and teachings of all world religions; and at a certain beginning stage one can be, for instance, both a practicing Buddhist and a practicing Christian. But if one pursues any path deeply enough, it eventually becomes necessary to embrace one spiritual path together with its underlying metaphysics.

Here, we can draw an analogy to the pursuit of education. We begin with a broad-based education; from grammar school perhaps through college, almost everyone initially studies a similar basic curriculum. But if we wish to pursue advanced training, perhaps a doctorate or some technical skill, we can do so only in a particular field. Likewise, from the point of view of the individual spiritual practitioner, as one goes deeper into one's spiritual path, practicing one religion and one truth becomes important. So, while it is essential that human society as a whole embrace the reality of many paths and many truths, for an individual, it may be better to follow one path and one truth.

CHAPTER 3

The Foundations of Buddhism

DEFINING FEATURES

As we have just seen, many religions provide valuable spiritual paths, but within individual experience, it is more effective to eventually focus on just one. So, I'll now begin to focus on the religion with which I have the most personal experience: Buddhism. First, let's examine where Buddhism can be found in relation to other world religions.

We can divide all world religions into two broad camps: the theistic ones, which assert the existence of a creator, and the nontheistic ones, which do not. Christianity, Judaism, Islam, and Hinduism are all examples of theistic religions. Buddhism, Jainism, and one branch of the ancient Indian tradition known as Samkhya are examples of nontheistic religions.

Within the nontheistic religions, we can again make two broad distinctions: there are those that assert the existence of *atman*, an eternal soul that is unitary, permanent, and unchanging, and those that do not. Buddhism is the sole example of the second division. In fact, the very rejection of an unchanging principle or an eternal soul is one of the main features distinguishing Buddhism from the other nontheistic traditions.

In looking at the ancient Indian spiritual traditions, we can also divide them another way: those that believe in rebirth and reincarnation, and those that do not. Within the former group, we can make another twofold division: those that, in addition to believing in rebirth, also believe in liberation from the cycle of rebirth, and those that do not. Buddhists believe in both rebirth and in the possibility of liberation, which we call *moksha* in Sanskrit.

Furthermore, among those who do accept the notion of liberation, there are those who understand attainment of liberation as reaching some other external plane of existence, and those who understand the attainment of liberation as the realization of a particular mental or spiritual state. Buddhism understands liberation from rebirth to be an attainment of a certain state of mind. Bearing all these distinctions in mind, the series of teachings I will present here constitutes the teachings of Buddhism.

THE BUDDHA

According to conventional understanding, the spiritual tradition that we know as Buddhism began its evolution more than 2,500 years ago. There is, however, a divergence of opinion among Buddhist scholars as to exactly when the historical Buddha, Siddhartha Gotama Shakyamuni, was born. Most Western scholars place his birth approximately 2,500 years ago; some Tibetan scholars such as the great Sakya Pandita argue that it has been more than 3,000 years since the Buddha came into the world; and there is still a third school of thought that maintains the Buddha lived 2,900 years ago.

As a Buddhist myself, I find this uncertainty about the precise dates of the life of Buddha Shakyamuni, the founder of the tradition, to be a bit embarrassing. I strongly feel that, out of deep reverence and respect, we should subject to close scientific scrutiny some of the authentic relics of the Buddha that are still available, and thereby clarify this matter significantly.

But leaving this detail aside, if we observe the life of Buddha Shakyamuni, we see that he went through a certain process of spiritual development. Born the son of a king, he was raised among all the palace luxuries. Eventually he gave up the comforts of his royal lifestyle, adopted an ascetic way of life, and went through a period of six years of severe spiritual practice. Later, he abandoned these ascetic practices as ultimately unsatisfactory and simply sat in meditation beneath a tree, which we call the *bodhi* tree, vowing not to rise until he attained enlightenment and liberation. As a result of this long and arduous process, he did eventually attain complete, unsurpassed, and perfect enlightenment.

The Buddha's life exemplifies a very important principle—a certain amount of hardship is necessary in one's spiritual pursuit. We can also see this principle at work in the lives of other great religious teachers, such as Jesus Christ or the Muslim prophet Mohammed. Furthermore, I think that the followers of these teachers, if they wish to attain the highest spiritual realizations within their tradition, must themselves undergo a process of hardship, which they endure through dedicated perseverance. There is sometimes the tendency among the followers of the Buddha to imagine, perhaps only in the back of their minds, that "Although the Buddha went through all of those hardships to attain enlightenment they aren't really necessary for *me*. Surely, *I* can attain enlightenment without giving up life's comforts." Perhaps such people imagine that, because they are somehow more fortunate than the Buddha, they can attain the same spiritual state as he did without any particular hardships or renunciation. This is, I think, mistaken.

Just as the Buddha adopted an ascetic lifestyle, leading the life of a true renunciate, the first disciples of the Buddha had a firm grounding for their spiritual practice within the framework of a celibate lifestyle. Because of this, throughout the history of Buddhism, the monastic community has played an important role in the dissemination and further development of the Buddha's teachings.

In addition to imagining that a certain degree of hardship and renunciation is unnecessary, certain people also mistakenly conclude that the moral and ethical teachings of Buddhism are also somehow superfluous to the "real" teachings of the Buddha. But, if we look closely, we see that each precept evolved from a teaching given by the Buddha about how to respond to a particular ethical challenge, a particular situation that arose in a follower's life. In this manner, eventually, all the ethical precepts and codes of conduct for the members of the monastic order evolved, and these in turn led to the adoption of a certain way of life, a life in accord with the teachings of the Buddha. Buddha also spoke extensively on philosophical topics meant to enhance his followers' practice and their understanding of the ethical precepts.

In this way, we see that the examples of the Buddha and his earliest disciples are relevant to our own spiritual path. While Buddhism has adapted to the culture of each new civilization it has encountered, it nonetheless retains its emphasis on morality and discipline as essential for spiritual maturation. If we ourselves want the attainments described by the Buddha—the deep concentration and the penetrating insights—then we too must endure some amount of hardship and observe ethical behavior.

The First Turning of the Wheel of Dharma

Shortly after attaining enlightenment under the bodhi tree, the Buddha gave a sermon in Varanasi sharing the fruits of his realization. This sermon is referred to as the "first turning of the wheel of Dharma." The word *Dharma* here refers to the Buddha's teachings themselves. It was this sermon in which the Buddha developed what would become the framework for the entirety of his teachings: the four noble truths.

These four truths are the truth of suffering, the truth of its origin, the truth of the possibility of its cessation, and the truth of the path that leads to that cessation. In essence, the four noble truths say that we all naturally desire happiness and do not wish to suffer—and that the suffering we wish to avoid comes about as a result of a chain of causes and conditions begun even before our birth. If we are to pursue our aspiration to gain freedom from suffering, we need to clearly understand the causes and conditions that give rise to suffering and strive to eliminate them. Additionally, we must clearly understand the causes and conditions that give rise to happiness as well, and actively practice them. This is the essence of the four noble truths.

Having established the framework of liberation in the four noble truths, the Buddha further detailed thirty-seven steps along the path to its attainment; these are called the thirty-seven aspects of the path to enlightenment. These aspects show specifically how the principles of the four noble truths are to be applied in one's day-to-day spiritual life. There are two primary components to these teachings: the cultivation of single-pointedness of mind, which is known as tranquil abiding *(shamata)*, and the cultivation of penetrative insight *(vipashyana)*. If we examine the thirty-seven aspects of the path to enlightenment in relation to these two qualities of mind, we find aspects relating to both qualities.

Of the thirty-seven aspects, the first four are the *four foundations of mindfulness:*

1. The foundation of mindfulness of the body,
2. The foundation of mindfulness of feelings,
3. The foundation of mindfulness of the mind, and
4. The foundation of mindfulness of phenomena.

As one deepens one's practice of these four foundations of mindfulness, one will develop greater enthusiasm for positive or "wholesome" activities. Thus, we have the second list, namely, the *four correct endeavors:*

5. Abandoning negative acts,
6. Preventing future negative acts,
7. Enhancing one's existing positive qualities and past wholesome acts, and
8. Laying the foundation for future wholesome acts.

Once the spiritual aspirant lays the solid foundations of mindfulness and ethical conduct, he or she will be able to further develop single-pointedness of mind, and thereby accomplish mental activities that cannot be sustained by a lesser degree of concentration.

Since these activities require a well-cultivated and unusually focused state of mind, they are called "supernatural." Therefore, the next four factors are the *four supernatural feats:*

9. The supernatural feat of aspiration,
10. The supernatural feat of joyous effort,
11. The supernatural feat of concentration, and
12. The supernatural feat of inquiry.

All of the first twelve factors relate to methods for enhancing one's capacity to remain focused single-pointedly on a chosen object of meditation. This enhanced capacity in turn leads to the enhancement of all of one's other positive spiritual faculties. Thus follow the *five faculties:*

13. The faculty of faith,
14. The faculty of joyous effort,
15. The faculty of mindfulness,
16. The faculty of meditative absorption, and
17. The faculty of wisdom or insight.

When these five faculties reach an advanced state, they become the *five powers:*

18. The power of faith,
19. The power of joyous effort,
20. The power of mindfulness,
21. The power of meditative absorption, and
22. The power of wisdom or insight.

When one develops these powers, one will naturally be able to follow the core of the Buddha's path, known as the *eightfold noble path*, which constitutes the next set, namely:

23. Right view,
24. Right thinking,
25. Right speech,
26. Right action,
27. Right livelihood,
28. Right effort,
29. Right mindfulness, and
30. Right concentration.

The final seven factors in this list are known as the *seven branches of enlightenment:*

31. The factor of enlightenment consisting of right mindfulness,
32. The factor of enlightenment consisting of right aspiration,
33. The factor of enlightenment consisting of right joyous effort,
34. The factor of enlightenment consisting of right joyfulness,
35. The factor of enlightenment consisting of right tranquility,
36. The factor of enlightenment consisting of right concentration, and
37. The factor of enlightenment consisting of right equanimity.

Together, the practice of the thirty-seven aspects of the path to enlightenment form the core of the practical application of the Buddha's teachings on the four noble truths and, therefore, of the Pali tradition of Buddhism. These, in turn can be said to be the foundations of Buddhism, and the first turning of the wheel of Dharma.

THE TWELVE LINKS OF DEPENDENT ORIGINATION

Fundamentally, the four noble truths are driven by the principle of causality; they manifest the law of cause and effect. The Buddha elaborates on the causal nature of the four truths with explanations of the twelve links of dependent origination.[3] At the root of these teachings on the twelve links is the assertion that all phenomena— our experience, things, and events—come into being as a result merely of the aggregation of causes and conditions. It is essential to clearly comprehend this teaching because, as we shall see, it forms the foundation for the Buddha's teaching on emptiness, the core teaching of the *Heart Sutra*. The twelve links of dependent origination are:

1. Ignorance,
2. Volitional Action,
3. Consciousness,
4. Name and Form,
5. Sense Sources,
6. Contact,
7. Feelings,
8. Attachment,
9. Grasping,
10. Becoming,
11. Birth, and
12. Aging and Death.

The sequential presentation of this causal chain, beginning with ignorance and proceeding through birth and death, describes the process of *unenlightened* existence. When we examine the cessation of phenomena, rather than their creation, the order is reversed, starting from the cessation of aging and death and moving backward through the cessation of birth, and so on. This reverse presentation describes the entire causal process of *enlightened* existence. Thus, the twelve links of dependent origination can describe the causal processes of both enlightened and unenlightened existence.

Through the twelve links of dependent origination, Buddha teaches that all things and all events, including all elements of one's individual experience, come into being merely as a result of the aggregation of causes and conditions. Understanding this, in turn, can lead us to see that all things are by nature interdependent, originating entirely as a result of other things and other factors.

Buddha teaches that the very fact that something is dependently originated means that it is necessarily devoid of an essential, or independent, reality. For if something is fundamentally *dependent*, by logical necessity it must be devoid of having a nature that is independent of other phenomena, of existing *independently*. Thus it is said that anything that is dependently originated must also be, in actual fact, empty.

One might wonder why this is so important; why does it matter that all phenomena are empty of any independent existence? It matters, Buddha teaches, because one who clearly understands the true nature of this emptiness will be liberated, released completely from all suffering. So how then do we go about understanding it? In the twelve links of dependent origination, it is said that the root of unenlightened existence lies in the first link, our basic ignorance of this empty nature of reality. Buddhist psychology contains many subtle and complex explanations of how to identify and overcome this ignorance, but essentially ignorance manifests itself in the way we experience emotional and mental afflictions. To really see how understanding ignorance will liberate us from suffering, we first need to examine these afflictions.

THE AFFLICTIONS

Much of Buddhist literature is devoted to exposing the nature of afflictions and the need to overcome them. In Sanskrit, the word for affliction is *klesha*, and the Tibetan equivalent is *nyon mong* (literally, "that which afflicts from within"). An affliction, by its very nature, brings about an immediate disturbance within the mind of the individual the moment it arises and thereby causes suffering within that individual.

When we speak in general of our aspiration to be happy and to be free from suffering, we are of course talking about our conscious experiences—that is, our wish to *experience* happiness and to not *experience* suffering. So, let us take a moment to examine the phenomenal nature of experience.

We can divide all conscious experience into two broad categories: sensory experience pertaining to the eye, ear, nose, tongue, and body; and experience of the mind itself. Sensory consciousness brings us experiences of physical pain, which we identify and experience as suffering, and experiences of physical pleasure, which we identify and experience as happiness. Our sensory consciousness can thus bring us a certain kind of suffering and happiness.

However, experiences of unhappiness and happiness at the level of *mental* consciousness are far more acute. If we look carefully, we see that much of our unhappiness and suffering is caused by disturbances in our thoughts and emotions. These are the result of the mental afflictions, the kleshas. Examples of these afflictions include attachment or greed, aversion or hatred, anger, pride, jealousy—the whole range of negative states a human being can experience. All these afflictions, as soon as they arise, immediately disturb our hearts and minds. Buddhist texts list many classes of afflictions, such as the six primary afflictions and the twenty derivative afflictions.[4]

If we carefully observe our experience, we can discover exactly what role mental afflictions play in our day-to-day lives. In observing our experience, we might think to ourselves, "Today I felt very peaceful and happy," or "Today I felt extremely restless and unhappy." The difference between these two cases is that in the first our mental state was less influenced by the mental afflictions, whereas in the latter case the afflictions were dominant. In truth, it is always and only the mental afflictions that agitate our minds, yet we tend to blame our agitation on external conditions, imagining that encountering unpleasant people or adverse circumstances makes us unhappy. However, as the great Indian Buddhist teacher Shantideva pointed out around the eighth century, when true practitioners of the Buddha's teaching encounter adversities, they remain resolute and unmoved, like a tree. Shantideva reminds us that encountering adversity, in itself, does not necessarily lead to a disturbed mind; even amid adversity, the principal cause of our unhappiness is our own undisciplined mind under the influence of the kleshas.[5] Failing to understand this principle, we allow ourselves to be controlled by the mental afflictions; in fact, we often embrace and reinforce them, for instance by adding fuel to our anger.

The mental afflictions are, by nature, relative and subjective; they have no absolute or objective basis. To see this more clearly, let us consider the example of food we find particularly unpleasant, particularly undesirable—perhaps the very sight of it disturbs us—and the afflictions of revulsion or disgust arise in our mind. If these afflictions have an absolute basis in objective reality, the qualities we experience—being repellent and disgusting—will be experienced in all circumstances by every person who encounters the food that possesses those qualities. That is to say, everyone will always react to this food with the same revulsion and disgust as we do. This is, of course, not the case.

People of one culture might find repugnant a food that people of another culture regard as a delicacy. We ourselves may even "develop a taste" for a food, thus learning to enjoy the experience of something we previously found unappetizing. All of this reveals that undesirability is something that we subjectively project; it does not exist intrinsically in any object or experience.

Let us look at another example. Everyone who is alive will age and die. The reality of aging and death is a simple fact of our existence and is beyond dispute. However, particularly in the West, many people are extremely reluctant to accept the reality of aging and death. This is so much the case that to even make the observation that someone is old is perceived to be unkind. Yet if we look at the attitudes of different societies, say, for example, of Tibetan society, the very same phenomena—aging and death—are seen in a radically different light. Advanced age is perceived to be a basis for greater respect. Thus, what from one cultural perspective is seen as negative is, from another, quite positive—but the phenomenon of aging itself has no intrinsic qualities in this regard.

From these examples, we can see the degree to which our own attitudes and perceptions make a difference in how we experience a given situation. Our attitudes reflect thoughts and emotions, and our thoughts and emotions reflect two principal drives: attraction and repulsion. If we perceive a thing, person, or event to be undesirable, we will react with repulsion and try to avoid it. This repulsion becomes the basis for hostility and other associated negative emotions. If, on the other hand, we find a thing, person, or event desirable, we will react with attraction and try to hold on to it. This attraction becomes the basis for craving and attachment. These basic dynamics of attraction and repulsion form the basis of our engagement with the world.

If we think along these lines, it will become clear that when we make statements such as "Today I feel happy" or "Today I feel unhappy," it is only emotions of attachment or aversion that determine which of these is the case. This doesn't mean that finding something desirable or undesirable is in itself an affliction. We have to examine the particular quality of that attraction or aversion.

All actions are actions of either body, speech, or mind. That is to say, every deed we commit is committed through something we do, say, or think. Buddhists refer to the actions created in this way as *karma*, which is simply the Sanskrit word for "action." All actions create consequences; Buddhists call this the *law of karma* or the *law of cause and effect*. As we have seen, the Buddha taught that we should cultivate actions with positive consequences (wholesome karma), while refraining from actions with negative consequences (unwholesome karma). Certain actions, such as those on the level of reflexes or biological processes, are entirely beyond conscious control and thus morally or karmicly neutral. However, our more significant actions necessarily stem from a motive or intention and are either destructive or helpful.

Destructive acts are motivated by disturbed states of mind, that is to say, by a mind dominated by the afflictions. In the entire history of human society, it is these mental afflictions, these undisciplined states of mind, that underlie all of humanity's destructive acts—from the smallest act of killing a fly to the greatest atrocities of war. We must remember that ignorance itself is an affliction: for example, when we fail to grasp the negative long-term consequences of an action and instead act out of shortsighted thoughts of gain.

If we closely examine feelings of strong desire or strong anger, we will find that at the root of these emotions lies our grasping at the object of these emotions. And, if we take it still further, we discover that at the root of all of this lies our grasping at a sense of self or ego. Not recognizing the emptiness of self and other, we mistakenly grasp at both as autonomous, objectively real, and independently existent.

As the eighth-century Indian philosopher Chandrakirti points out in his *Guide to the Middle Way*, we first grasp at a sense of self, and then we extend that grasping onto others. First you have a sense of "I," then you grasp at things as "mine." By looking into our own minds, we can see that the stronger our grasping is, the more forcefully it generates negative and destructive emotions. There is a very intimate causal connection between our grasping at a sense of self and the arising of destructive emotions within us. As long as we remain under the dominion of this erroneous belief, we have no room for lasting joy—this is what it means to be imprisoned in the cycle of existence. Suffering is nothing but existence enslaved to ignorance.

Although there are many afflictions, and many ways of classifying them, three in particular—attachment, anger, and delusion—are often referred to as the *three poisons* of the mind. Just as poison causes harm to the body and physical suffering and can even bring one's life to an end, these mental afflictions also cause us intense misery—perhaps even hastening our death.

Ultimately, mental afflictions not only cause suffering to ourselves and others, but they also obstruct our attainment of happiness. In this sense, these internal states are our true enemy. These internal enemies are even more pernicious than any external enemy ever could be. Although we might at least stand a chance of hiding from an external enemy, no matter where we may go, mental afflictions can arise. Furthermore, the internal enemy always remains our enemy; there is not even the slightest chance that our internal enemies might become our friends at some point in the future. There is no place to which one can escape the internal enemy, no way to win the enemy over to our side, and no way the enemy will cease its attack. So what can we do?

Abandoning the Causes of Suffering

By understanding emptiness, by clearly perceiving the empty nature of all phenomena, including ourselves, we can liberate ourselves from negative emotions, and thus from the creation of unwholesome karma and the power of the internal enemy. Through this process, we can begin to undo the harm we've caused by our grasping, and the derivative strong emotions to which it gives rise. The moment we begin to develop insight into the empty nature of self and all reality, the process of releasing our deluded grasp begins. At the moment of our first insight into the empty nature of self and reality, we start to break free of the enslavement of ignorance and the attack of the internal enemy. By reducing our grasping, we start to undo the causal chain of unenlightened existence. By undermining self-grasping ignorance, the first link of dependent origination, you prevent the arising of the second link, and ultimately become free of the endless cycle of suffering lifetimes.

But what does all this mean exactly? If we arrive at the knowledge that the self at which we grasp is empty, we may imagine this means that we as individuals with personal identities do not exist. But of course this is not the case—our own personal experiences demonstrate that as subjects and agents of our own lives, we certainly exist. So how, then, do we understand the content of this insight into absence of self? What follows from this insight? We must be very clear that *only the self that is being grasped as intrinsically real* needs to be negated. The self as a conventional phenomenon is not rejected. This is a crucial aspect of the Buddha's teachings on emptiness. Without understanding this distinction, one cannot fully understand the meaning of no-self. Later on, as we get more deeply into the discussion of the *Heart Sutra,* I will elaborate on this point in greater detail.

How then do we cultivate a clear understanding of emptiness? In order to practice the Buddhist path, we need to generate a deep sense of renunciation of the very nature of our present existence, which is characterized by mental and physical aggregates under the control of karma and afflictions. Not only is this unenlightened existence the consequence of past delusions and mental afflictions, but it acts as the basis for both our present and future experiences of suffering and afflictions as well. We must therefore develop a deep aspiration to gain freedom from this conditioned existence.

The heart of renunciation is a quest for a victory over the internal enemy, the mental afflictions.

In this context, "renunciation" does not refer to the act of giving up all our possessions, but rather to a state of mind. As long as our minds continue to be driven by ignorance, there is no room for lasting happiness, and we remain susceptible to problem after problem. To cut through this cycle, we need to understand the nature of this suffering of conditioned existence and cultivate a strong wish to gain freedom from it. This is true renunciation.

The endless cycle of suffering, of enduring countless rounds of birth and death, is called *samsara*. We renounce samsara in order to attain nirvana. *Nirvana* literally means "the state beyond sorrows" and refers to the state of freedom from cyclic existence. The "sorrows" beyond which nirvana lies are the mental afflictions. We therefore take refuge in the various spiritual states that we cultivate in order to directly counteract negative mental states; it is these that protect us from the afflictions. And, ultimately, it is in the state free from the mental afflictions that we take our final refuge; this is the true Dharma.

When trying to eliminate the mental afflictions gradually, we first combat the gross levels and then proceed on to the more subtle ones. Aryadeva, a third-century Indian master, presents three stages for overcoming the mental afflictions in his *Four Hundred Verses on the Middle Way*. He writes:

First, the unwholesome must be averted.
In the middle, the self must be averted.
Last, all the views are averted.
Wise is the one who knows this.[6]

The first stage of spiritual practice is to restrain oneself from gross negative actions of body, speech, and mind, such as the ten unwholesome actions.[7] In the second stage, once one has gained a certain degree of restraint regarding these actions, one challenges the afflictions directly by means of applying antidotes. For example, to counter anger, one cultivates lovingkindness, and to counter attachment, one contemplates impermanence. These antidotes help to reduce the intensity of negative emotions. However, the most direct method for overcoming the mental afflictions is to cultivate insight into emptiness. In this final stage, one strives to eliminate not only the afflictions, but also the propensities that are their residue, so that no trace remains that can bring about future occurrence of these afflictions.

In summary, ignorance lies at the root of all the afflictions, and the afflictions are inevitably at the root of suffering. Ignorance and afflictions are known as the true origins of suffering, and their effects are known as true suffering. Insight into emptiness is the true path. And, finally, the freedom that we attain through cultivation of this wisdom is true cessation.

CHAPTER 4

The Great Vehicle

THE MAHAYANA SCHOOL

IN ORDER TO FULLY UNDERSTAND the *Heart Sutra*, we must understand its place within the entire canon of Buddhist literature. The *Heart Sutra* is part of the Perfection of Wisdom literature, which is composed of distinctly Mahayana ("Great Vehicle") texts. These Mahayana texts form the core of the "second turning of the wheel of Dharma." The Mahayana teachings are rooted in the sermons that the Buddha taught primarily at Vulture Peak. Whereas the teachings of the first turning emphasize suffering and its cessation, the teachings of the second turning emphasize emptiness.

In the Mahayana school there are also teachings that come from the "third turning of the wheel of Dharma." Within these, we can speak of two categories of scriptures: those scriptures that present an interpretive reading of the Perfection of Wisdom sutras, and those that present the theory of buddha nature (the Sanskrit word for this nature is *tathagatagarbha*). Because the Perfection of Wisdom literature emphasizes emptiness, the interpretative readings of them in the third turning were taught primarily for the benefit of spiritual practitioners who, although inclined toward the Mahayana path, are not yet ready to properly make use of Buddha's teachings on the emptiness of inherent existence. If such trainees were to embrace the apparent literal meaning of the Perfection of Wisdom sutras before seeing into the Buddha's true meaning, they would be in danger of falling into the extreme of nihilism. It is important to know that the Buddha's teachings are most certainly not nihilistic as that term is understood by philosophers, nor does the Buddha's teaching on the emptiness of inherent existence entail mere nonexistence.

One way of avoiding the extreme of nihilism is by contextualizing emptiness in terms of specific phenomena. For instance, in the *Sutra Unraveling the Thought of the Buddha (Samdhinirmochana Sutra)*, the Buddha offers a way of understanding the Perfection of Wisdom sutras by contextualizing the notion of "identitylessness."[8]

NAGARJUNA AND THE GREAT VEHICLE

Although the Tibetan tradition attributes the origin of the Mahayana teachings to the Buddha himself, scholars from other sects have historically expressed doubts on this matter, and some contemporary scholars do so as well. It seems that even before the time of Nagarjuna (a great Buddhist teacher in India who lived around the second century C.E.) there were contrasting opinions about this. Consequently, we find in Nagarjuna's writings, such as the *Precious Garland (Ratnavali)*, an entire section in which Nagarjuna attempts to prove the authenticity of the Mahayana sutras. We also find such arguments in Maitreya's *Ornament of Mahayana Sutras (Mahayana Sutralamkara)*, in Shantideva's *Guide to the Bodhisattva's Way of Life (Bodhicharyavatara)*, and in Bhavaviveka's *Essence of the Middle Way (Madhyamakahridaya)*.

For our purposes, let's examine the core of Nagarjuna's argument: If the path taught in the first turning of the wheel—the thirty-seven aspects of the path to enlightenment—were the only path to enlightenment taught by the Buddha, then there would be no substantial difference between the spiritual process leading to the full enlightenment of a buddha and that leading to the individual liberation attained by an arhat. Another way of saying this would be that an individual who attained nirvana (the elimination of one's own suffering) would be identical in understanding and abilities to one who attained the complete enlightenment of a buddha. If it is the case that these two states are identical, then the only substantial difference between them would be the time it takes to attain them: In order to attain buddhahood one must accumulate merit for three innumerable eons, whereas the individual liberation of an arhat can be attained far more quickly. Nagarjuna argues, however, that such a position (that the states are identical but for the time involved) is untenable.

Nagarjuna points out that one of the metaphysical ideas current in the earlier Buddhist traditions is that at the time of the Buddha's final nirvana, which is known as "nirvana without residue"—conventionally, the point of death—the continuum of the being comes to an end. If this were the case, he argues, then the period of time during which Buddha Shakyamuni was able to work for the welfare of other sentient beings following his full awakening, which was his primary reason for accumulating merit and wisdom over three innumerable eons, was extraordinarily short. The Buddha left his royal life at the age of twenty-nine, attained full enlightenment at the age of thirty-six, and passed away at the age of eighty or eighty-one. This would imply that the Buddha was able to work for the benefit of other sentient beings for only a few decades. For Nagarjuna, this huge disparity between the duration of the Buddha's training and the duration of his activity after enlightenment does not make sense.

He further argues that there is no basis for positing that the continuum of an individual's mind would come to an end upon the attainment of final nirvana, because there is nothing that can bring about the total cessation of the continuum of consciousness. He asserts that if there is a sufficient antidote to any given phenomenon or event, then that antidote can be said to cause the complete cessation of the functioning of that phenomenon or event. (For example, a sufficient antidote of a bodily poison would cause the complete cessation of the functioning of that poison.) However, insofar as continuum of consciousness itself is concerned, no event or an agent can bring about its total destruction. Nagarjuna argues that the innate mind and the defilements or afflictions that obscure its inherent clarity are two separate things. Mental pollutants— defilements and afflictions—can be eliminated by practicing the powerful antidotes of the Buddha's teachings. However, the continuum of the mind itself remains endless.

Nagarjuna claims that not only are the teachings found in the Sanskrit Mahayana tradition more profound than the teachings of the Pali tradition, but also that they do not contradict the Pali teachings. In a sense, one could say that the Mahayana scriptures elaborate on themes presented and first developed in the earlier teachings of the Buddha, giving deeper and more detailed explanations of the ideas presented there. In this manner, Nagarjuna argues the authenticity of the Mahayana teachings.

There is a process of reflection in the Sakya teachings of the Path and Fruition (*Lamdré*) that is helpful in determining the validity of teachings. This tradition speaks of *four valid sources of knowledge:* the valid scriptures of the Buddha, the valid commentaries, the valid teacher, and one's own valid experience. In terms of the historical evolution of these four factors, one can say that the valid scriptures, those taught by the Buddha, came into being first. Based upon the reading and interpretation of these scriptures, many valid commentaries and treatises evolved, explaining the most profound meaning of the Buddha's teachings. Nagarjuna's work is an example of this. Then, based upon the study and practice of these valid commentaries, certain practitioners may have mastered or actualized the themes presented in the scriptures and their commentaries, and thereby become valid teachers. Finally, on the basis of the teachings given by such teachers, valid experience or realization grows in the hearts of practitioners.

However, one becomes able to personally verify the validity of these four sources in a different order than that in which the sources historically evolved: in order to develop deep conviction in the validity of the Buddha's teachings, one first needs a degree of experience of them. Thus one's own valid experience becomes the first factor. When we speak of valid experience, there can be ordinary valid experiences and special ones. Although we may not possess extraordinary kinds of spiritual experiences at present, we can all attain ordinary types of spiritual experience. For example, when we reflect deeply upon the teachings on compassion, we can feel some impact in our minds and in our hearts—we feel aroused and experience a deep sense of unbearableness. Similarly, when we reflect on the teachings on emptiness and no-self, it may bring about a deeper impact within us. These are spiritual experiences.

Once one has such spiritual experiences, even at an ordinary level, one has a taste of what it feels like to truly have these realizations. Based on that little experience, one can more meaningfully be convinced of the validity of the great spiritual realizations that are talked about in the sutras, in the commentaries, and in the biographies of the masters. This process of beginning with our own experience and using it to verify the teachings and the teachers is quite important; one could say, in fact, that this is the only way open to us.

In *Fundamentals of the Middle Way*, Nagarjuna pays homage to the Buddha as a valid teacher who taught the ultimate nature of reality, who embodies the principle of great compassion, and who, acting exclusively through the power of his compassion for all sentient beings, has revealed the path that will lead to the overcoming of all erroneous views. Reflecting deeply upon our own experience, we will become able to validate what Nagarjuna says for ourselves and make our own determination of the authenticity of the Mahayana teachings.

ORIGINS OF THE GREAT VEHICLE

After the Buddha's death, his teachings were compiled by some of his principal disciples. This compilation actually happened at three different points in time. It is certain that the Mahayana scriptures were not part of the three compilations that today constitute what is known as the Pali canon. Furthermore, when we examine the Mahayana scriptures themselves, we find statements that seem problematic in various ways. For example, the Perfection of Wisdom sutras state that they were taught by the Buddha at Vulture Peak in Rajagriha to a vast congregation of disciples. However, if you have visited the site in present-day Rajgir, it is obvious that it is impossible for more than a few people to fit onto the summit. So, we have to understand the truth of these accounts at a different level, a level beyond the ordinary one confined by conventional notions of space and time.

Nagarjuna and Asanga (another great Indian teacher, who lived in the fourth century C.E.) played a critical role in the compilation of the Mahayana scriptures. They are identified as its principal custodians and interpreters. However, there is a gap of at least four hundred years between the death of the Buddha and the birth of Nagarjuna, and perhaps as many as nine hundred years difference between the Buddha's death and the birth of Asanga. We might therefore ask what it is that ensures that the Mahayana scriptures were indeed continually transmitted from the time of the Buddha to the times of Nagarjuna and Asanga. In the Mahayana scriptures, that link is the bodhisattvas, such as Maitreya and Manjushri. It is said that, in the case of Nagarjuna, it is the bodhisattva Manjushri who transmits the lineage. Bhavaviveka explicitly states in his text *The Blaze of Reasoning (Tarkajvala)* that the great bodhisattvas compiled the Mahayana scriptures. These accounts create a rather complex picture.

How are we to understand these statements about the origins of the Mahayana scriptures in relation to conventional notions of time? We can probably say that the Mahayana scriptures were not taught by the historical Buddha to the general public in any conventional sense.

Furthermore, it may be the case that Mahayana scriptures, such as the Perfection of Wisdom sutras, were taught to a group of a few individuals whom the Buddha regarded as most suited to receive those teachings. This accords with the Buddhist assertion that a buddha transmits teachings in ways tailored to the diverse aptitudes and diverse physiological and psychological states of practitioners.

Thus, in this context, the teachings may have been transmitted on a plane that transcends conventional understandings of time and space. In this way, we may understand the origin of Mahayana texts, and the origin of the *Heart Sutra*.

CHAPTER 5

Freedom from Suffering

SUFFERING AND COMPASSION

REGARDLESS of its historical origin and its evolution, the Mahayana is without a doubt a path dedicated to the liberation of all beings. When one enters the Mahayana path, one is said to join the family of bodhisattvas. This happens when anyone has, in the course of their spiritual development, gained the realization of genuine compassion. Compassion can of course be understood on many levels, and at the highest level compassion ultimately liberates you, but let's examine what is meant here by "genuine compassion."

According to Buddhism, compassion is an aspiration, a state of mind, wanting others to be free from suffering. It's not passive—it's not empathy alone—but rather an empathetic altruism that actively strives to free others from suffering. Genuine compassion must have both wisdom and lovingkindness. That is to say, one must understand the nature of the suffering from which we wish to free others (this is wisdom), and one must experience deep intimacy and empathy with other sentient beings (this is lovingkindness). Let's examine these two elements.

The suffering from which we wish to liberate other sentient beings, according to Buddha's teachings, has three levels. The first level includes the obvious physical and mental sensations of pain and discomfort that we can all easily identify as suffering. This kind of suffering is primarily at the sensory level—unpleasant or painful sensations and feelings. The great Tibetan master Panchen Losang Chokyi Gyaltsan, tutor to the fifth Dalai Lama, reminds us that even animals seek to avoid physical suffering and pain.

The second level of suffering is the suffering of change. Although certain experiences or sensations may seem pleasurable and desirable now, inherent within them is the potential for culminating in an unsatisfactory experience. Another way of saying this is that experiences do not last forever; desirable experiences will eventually be replaced by a neutral experience or an undesirable experience. If it were not the case that desirable experiences are of the nature of change, then, once having a happy experience, we would remain happy forever! In fact, if desirability were intrinsic to an experience, then the longer we remained in contact with it, the happier we would become. However, this is not the case. In fact, often, the more we pursue these experiences, the greater our level of disillusionment, dissatisfaction, and unhappiness becomes.

We can probably find numerous examples of the suffering of change in our lives, but here let us take for example the simple case of someone who buys a new car. For the first few days, the person may be completely happy, utterly pleased with the purchase, constantly thinking about the car, mindfully and lovingly dusting it and cleaning it and polishing it. The person may even feel that he wants to sleep next to it! As time passes, however, the level of excitement and joy is no longer quite as high. Perhaps the person begins to take the car more for granted, or perhaps he begins to regret that he didn't get the more expensive model or a different color. Gradually, the level of pleasure from owning the car diminishes, culminating eventually in some form of dissatisfaction—perhaps a desire for another, newer car. That's what we Buddhists mean when we talk about the suffering of change.

The spiritual practitioner needs to cultivate awareness and recognition of this level of suffering. Awareness of this level of suffering is not unique to Buddhists; the aspiration to gain freedom from the suffering of change can be found among non-Buddhist practitioners of meditative absorption.

But the third level of suffering is the most significant—the pervasive suffering of conditioning. This refers to the very fact of our unenlightened existence, the fact that we are ruled by negative emotions and their underlying root cause, namely our own fundamental ignorance of the nature of reality. Buddhism asserts that as long as we are under the control of this fundamental ignorance, we are suffering; this unenlightened existence is suffering by its very nature.

If we are to cultivate the deepest wisdom, we must understand suffering at its deepest, most pervasive level. In turn, freedom from that level of suffering is true nirvana, true liberation, the true state of cessation. Freedom from the first level of suffering alone— merely being free of unpleasant physical and psychological experiences—is not true cessation of suffering. Freedom from the second level is again not true cessation. However, freedom from the third level of suffering—being completely free from the very source of suffering—that is genuine cessation, genuine liberation.

It is said that freedom from the first level of suffering is attained to some degree by attaining higher rebirths—a more fortunate human rebirth, or rebirth as a long-lived god. Freedom from the second level of suffering can be attained through mundane meditative states. For instance, through the practice of deep meditative absorption, an individual can experience what are called the four form realms and the four formless realms. In the highest form realm and in all four formless realms, sentient beings are said to be free from sensations of both pain and pleasure and remain in a neutral state of feeling—but these states do not extend beyond the period one is in deep meditative absorption. Thus, without escaping cyclic existence, there are realms in which one can gain freedom from both the first and second levels of suffering. Freedom from the third level of suffering is the true Dharma, which protects us from *all* suffering and negativity. And the path leading to that Dharma is called the Buddha's way.

Understanding suffering in this way is the first element of genuine compassion. The second element of genuine compassion, lovingkindness, developing a feeling of intimacy with and empathy toward all beings, must be accomplished on the basis of recognizing our interconnectedness and interdependence with them. We must develop a capacity to connect with others, to feel close to others. This can be accomplished by consciously and intentionally recollecting the limitations and the harmful consequences of self-cherishing—cherishing only one's own well-being—and then reflecting upon the virtues and merits of cherishing the well-being of others. In chapter 12, I will explain in more depth some practices for generating compassion and the altruistic attitude called *bodhichitta*.

Integrating All the Teachings

As we prepare to examine the *Heart Sutra* in depth, let me point out that in reading the Perfection of Wisdom sutras, there exists a tradition of interpretation whereby one understands the subject matter of these teachings on two different levels. On one hand, there is the explicit subject matter, which is Buddha's teaching on emptiness; on the other hand, there is the hidden subject matter, which relates to the stages of the path associated with the deepening levels of understanding of emptiness. The Perfection of Wisdom scriptures explicitly present the teachings of emptiness in great detail through enumeration of various categories of phenomena, both impure (such as the five aggregates) and pure (such as the four noble truths). At the same time, these scriptures implicitly present the stages of the path to enlightenment in terms of progressive levels of insight into emptiness.[9]

As I have said, the first turning of the wheel of Dharma lays down the basic structure of the Buddha's path to enlightenment within the framework of the four noble truths. The second turning of the wheel, comprised principally of the Perfection of Wisdom texts, further elaborates on the third noble truth, the truth of cessation, particularly in terms of understanding the ultimate nature of reality, emptiness. As one's understanding of the ultimate nature of reality deepens, one begins to recognize more clearly the erroneous nature of one's belief in intrinsic existence. As the erroneous nature of this belief becomes increasingly evident, one's insight into the true nature of reality becomes deeper and clearer. In this way, we also lay a foundation for the deeper understanding of the subjective experience of emptiness, which is the key theme in the third turning of the wheel of Dharma. The principal scriptures of the third turning are the *Buddha Nature Sutra* (*Tathagata-garbhasutra*), which is the basis of Maitreya's *Sublime Continuum* (*Uttaratantra*) and Nagarjuna's *Collection of Hymns*. These scriptures present, in great detail, the teachings of buddha nature and the nature of the subjective experience of emptiness, and thereby lay the foundations for the Vajrayana, or tantra, teachings. When viewed in this way, we see that the earlier teachings of the Buddha laid a foundation for the later teachings, and that later teachings enhance and elaborate on themes touched upon in the earlier teachings, thereby complementing them.

Understood thusly, one can see that the form of Buddhism that flourished in Tibet is a comprehensive form of Buddhism, embracing all the essential teachings of the Theravada, the Mahayana, and the Vajrayana scriptures. It is very important to understand that the core teachings of the Theravada tradition embodied in the Pali scriptures are the foundation of the Buddha's teachings. Beginning with these teachings, one can then draw on the insights contained in the detailed explanations of the Sanskrit Mahayana tradition. Finally, integrating techniques and perspectives from the Vajrayana texts can further enhance one's understanding. But without a foundation in the core teachings embodied in the Pali tradition, simply proclaiming oneself a follower of the Mahayana is meaningless.[10]

If one has this kind of deeper understanding of various scriptures and their interpretation, one is spared from harboring mistaken notions of conflicts between the "Greater" versus the "Lesser" Vehicle *(Hinayana)*. Sometimes there is a regrettable tendency on the part of certain followers of the Mahayana to disparage the teachings of the Theravada, claiming that they are the teachings of the Lesser Vehicle, and thereby not suited to one's own personal practice. Similarly, on the part of followers of the Pali tradition, there is sometimes a tendency to reject the validity of the Mahayana teachings, claiming they are not actually the Buddha's teachings. As we move into our examination of the *Heart Sutra,* what is important is to understand deeply how these traditions complement each other and to see how, at the individual level, each of us can integrate all these core teachings into our personal practice.

Part II

The Heart Sutra

The Text of the Heart Sutra

The Blessed Mother, the Heart of the Perfection of Wisdom[11]

IN SANSKRIT: *Bhagavati Prajna Paramita Hridaya*

[This is the first segment.][12]

THUS HAVE I ONCE HEARD:

The Blessed One was staying in Rajgriha at Vulture Peak along with a great community of monks and a great community of bodhisattvas, and at that time, the Blessed One entered the meditative absorption on the varieties of phenomena called the appearance of the profound. At that time as well, the noble Avalokiteshvara, the bodhisattva, the great being, clearly beheld the practice of the profound perfection of wisdom itself and saw that even the five aggregates are empty of intrinsic existence.

Thereupon, through the Buddha's inspiration, the venerable Shariputra spoke to the noble Avalokiteshvara, the bodhisattva, the great being, and said, "How should any noble son or noble daughter who wishes to engage in the practice of the profound perfection of wisdom train?"

When this had been said, the holy Avalokiteshvara, the bodhisattva, the great being, spoke to the venerable Shariputra and said, "Shariputra, any noble son or noble daughter who so wishes to engage in the practice of the profound perfection of wisdom should clearly see this way: they should see perfectly that even the five aggregates are empty of intrinsic existence. Form is emptiness, emptiness is form; emptiness is not other than form, form too is not other than emptiness. Likewise, feelings, perceptions, mental formations, and consciousness are all empty. Therefore, Shariputra, all phenomena are emptiness; they are without defining characteristics; they are not born, they do not cease; they are not defiled, they are not undefiled; they are not deficient, and they are not complete.

"Therefore, Shariputra, in emptiness there is no form, no feelings, no perceptions, no mental formations, and no consciousness. There is no eye, no ear, no nose, no tongue, no body, and no mind. There is no form, no sound, no smell, no taste, no texture, and no mental objects. There is no eye-element and so on up to no mind-element including up to no element of mental consciousness. There is no ignorance, there is no extinction of ignorance, and so on up to no aging and death and no extinction of aging and death. Likewise, there is no suffering, origin, cessation, or path; there is no wisdom, no attainment, and even no non-attainment.

"Therefore, Shariputra, since bodhisattvas have no attainments, they rely on this perfection of wisdom and abide in it. Having no obscuration in their minds, they have no fear, and by going utterly beyond error, they will reach the end of nirvana. All the buddhas too who abide in the three times attained the full awakening of unexcelled, perfect enlightenment by relying on this profound perfection of wisdom.

"Therefore, one should know that the mantra of the perfection of wisdom—the mantra of great knowledge, the unexcelled mantra, the mantra equal to the unequalled, the mantra that quells all suffering—is true because it is not deceptive. The mantra of the perfection of wisdom is proclaimed:

tadyatha gaté gaté paragaté parasamgaté bodhi svaha!

Shariputra, the bodhisattvas, the great beings, should train in the perfection of wisdom in this way."

Thereupon, the Blessed One arose from that meditative absorption and commended the holy Avalokiteshvara, the bodhisattva, the great being, saying this is excellent. "Excellent! Excellent! O noble child, it is just so; it should be just so. One must practice the profound perfection of wisdom just as you have revealed. For then even the tathagatas will rejoice."

As the Blessed One uttered these words, the venerable Shariputra, the holy Avalokiteshvara, the bodhisattva, the great being, along with the entire assembly, including the worlds of gods, humans, asuras, and gandharvas, all rejoiced and hailed what the Blessed One had said.

CHAPTER 6

The Opening

THE PERFECTION OF WISDOM SUTRAS

IT IS SAID there are eighty-four thousand collections of discourses, which the Buddha taught to accord with the diverse mental dispositions and spiritual inclinations of sentient beings. The Perfection of Wisdom literature, the *Prajnaparamita*, is the principal genre among them. It is part of the Sanskrit Buddhist tradition and includes the *Heart Sutra*, also called the *Heart of Wisdom Sutra*, which we will be examining here in depth. Emphasizing the Mahayana ideal of the bodhisattva who aspires to liberate all beings, these Perfection of Wisdom sutras flourished in many countries, including China—from where they were brought to Japan, Korea, and Vietnam—and Tibet, from where they were transmitted to Mongolia, to the vast expanse of the trans-Himalayan region, and to areas within the Russian federation. In the forms of Buddhism that developed in all of these countries, the *Heart Sutra* plays an important role—in fact, in many cases, a practitioner may recite it daily.

In Tibet, the Perfection of Wisdom sutras also became an important subject for scholarly discourse in the monastic colleges. A monk would spend an average of five to seven years studying these sutras in depth. Furthermore, the monastic student would also study many commentaries on these sutras; there are at least twenty-one Indian commentaries that were translated into Tibetan and many more that originated in Tibet itself. The study of the Perfection of Wisdom sutras is emphasized in all four schools of Tibetan Buddhism—Nyingma, Sakya, Kagyu, and Geluk.

We can see these sutras' importance in a story about the famous eighteenth-century Tibetan scholar and adept Jamyang Shepa, who was both an acclaimed writer and a highly realized practitioner. At one point, he was challenged by a questioner who said, "You have a great reputation as a master of the Perfection of Wisdom literature. Does that mean that your expertise in other fields, like Middle Way *(Madhyamaka)* philosophy, is not so great?" Jamyang Shepa responded by stating that if one examines Madhyamaka philosophy, it represents the philosophical standpoint of the Perfection of Wisdom sutras; if one examines the study of epistemology, it represents the methods of inquiry that are essentially a medium for understanding the Perfection of Wisdom; if one examines the *Vinaya* (the monastic discipline), it presents the precepts that the practitioner of the Perfection of Wisdom must undertake; and if one examines the Abhidharma, one finds that its taxonomy of reality is central to the Perfection of Wisdom sutras. Thus, Jamyang Shepa asserted that the Perfection of Wisdom is the foundation of all the other fields of study.

Generally speaking, there are many different texts within the Perfection of Wisdom sutras. Those that were translated into Tibetan are collectively known as the *seventeen mother and son scriptures.* The *Heart Sutra* is one among these seventeen, and is sometimes also known as the *Twenty-Five Verses on the Perfection of Wisdom.*

There are somewhat different versions of the *Heart Sutra*; for instance, there seems to be a slight variance between the Tibetan and Chinese versions. In the Chinese version, the text begins with the presentation of the teaching on emptiness, whereas the Tibetan version has a preliminary section describing the context in which the Buddha first gave this teaching. Also, as with the Tibetan version, the Chinese version gives a presentation of emptiness in terms of what is known as the "fourfold emptiness," while I've been told that the Japanese version presents a "sixfold emptiness." For our purposes in this book, we will use the Tibetan version of the *Heart of Wisdom Sutra*.

In Tibetan Buddhism, before beginning a teaching such as this, it is traditional to say how one has received the lineage transmission of the text. I have received the oral transmission of this important scripture. However, the lineage for the transmission of its commentary does not survive today. I have, however, received surviving transmissions of commentaries on other Perfection of Wisdom sutras, such as the *Eight Thousand Verse Perfection of Wisdom*.

GIVING THE TITLE AND PAYING HOMAGE

The Blessed Mother, the Heart of the Perfection of Wisdom
In Sanskrit: *Bhagavati Prajna Paramita Hridaya*

The *Heart Sutra* begins with the statement of its title. Even in the Tibetan text, this includes a statement of the title in Sanskrit: *Bhagavati Prajna Paramita Hridaya*. Giving the Sanskrit title at the beginning of a Tibetan text serves to indicate that its origin is authentic. It also demonstrates the tremendous respect that Tibetans traditionally have for texts translated from the Indian language and for the Indian tradition itself.

Buddhism in Tibet began around the seventh century. At that time, the Tibetan monarch Songtsen Gampo had as one of his queens a Chinese princess, Wen-ching, whose influence contributed to bringing Chinese Buddhism to Tibet. Yet, despite Wen-ching's influence through Songtsen Gampo, the primary transmission of Buddhism into Tibet came directly from India.

This fact is evident if we look at the corpus of the Tibetan canon. There are over one hundred volumes of *Kangyur*—translations of sacred words—which are all attributed to the Buddha. There are over two hundred volumes of *Tengyur*—translations of treatises—which represent the collection of authentic commentaries. In this collection of more than three hundred large volumes, there are just a few volumes containing translations from Chinese sources, one of which is the well-known commentary on the *Sutra Unraveling the Thought of the Buddha (Samdhinirmochanasutra)*. There are also a few texts on Vinaya, the monastic discipline, translated from Pali sources. But with the exception of these few texts, the entire Tibetan Buddhist canon was translated into Tibetan from Sanskrit.

Scholars agree that the Tibetan translations of Indian sources are very faithful with regard to the originals. Over time, Tibetan and Chinese became the two most important non-Indian languages through which Mahayana Buddhism was transmitted from country to country, giving rise to the numerous other varieties of Mahayana Buddhism. From the Chinese-language tradition of Buddhism evolved other varieties of Buddhism in East Asia, while from the Tibetan-language scriptures evolved Mongolian Buddhism and the

Buddhism found in the trans-Himalayan region. Today, Tibetan remains one of the most important living languages through which the practices and teachings related to the bodhisattva vehicle can be accurately transmitted.

The Tibetan text of the *Heart Sutra* title reads, "The Heart of the Perfection of Wisdom, the Bhagavati." The term *Bhagavati* has the connotation of "mother." Thus, the Perfection of Wisdom is likened to a mother who gives birth to the *aryas*, or noble beings. Perfection of Wisdom in the title indicates the subject matter of the text. The term *heart* suggests that, among the vast corpus of the Perfection of Wisdom sutras, the text at hand is the pith—a concise presentation of the teachings elaborated upon in the rest of the Perfection of Wisdom sutras. This sutra lies, as at were, at the heart of these teachings.

In the Tibetan version of the text, the translator pays homage to the mother, the Perfection of Wisdom. Sometime after this translation was made, a custom evolved in Tibet, established at one point by royal decree, for translators to choose specific entities to which to pay homage at the beginning of a text that they were translating. This dedication served to identify which of the three scriptural collections—Abhidharma, Sutra, or Vinaya—the work at hand belonged. If the text belonged to the Abhidharma collection—the subtle teachings of Buddhist psychology—then homage was paid to Manjushri, who is seen as the embodiment of knowledge and wisdom. If the text belonged to the Sutra collection, homage was paid to all the buddhas and bodhisattvas. If the text belonged to the Vinaya, then homage was paid to the omniscient mind of the Buddha. Through this custom, it was easy to identify which text belonged to which category.

In the Tibetan text of the *Heart Sutra*, immediately after the translator's homage, there is a simple statement: "This is the first segment." In general, the segments were identified in this way to help ensure that in the future no corruption, such as additions or omissions in transcription, would occur in the text. Since the *Heart Sutra* is a short text, with a length equivalent to twenty-five verses, it is designated as having only a single segment.

The Origin of the Teaching

The main body of the text begins by presenting the context, the background to the occurrence of this teaching. In fact, there are two different contexts: the common context, which gives an account of the teaching's worldly origin, and the uncommon context, which presents an account of the teaching's ultimate origin. Regarding the common context, the text reads:

> Thus have I once heard: The Blessed One was staying in Rajgriha at Vulture Peak along with a great community of monks and a great community of bodhisattvas, and at that time, the Blessed One entered the meditative absorption on the varieties of phenomena called the appearance of the profound.

Thus, the text indicates that three conditions, called *perfect conditions,* have come together: the presence of the perfect teacher, here Buddha Shakyamuni; the presence of a perfect congregation of listeners, here consisting of a great community of monks and bodhisattvas; the coming together of these first two conditions at a perfect location, here Vulture Peak at Rajagriha. "Great community of monks" here refers to the ultimate sangha, such as the great arhats.

With regard to the uncommon context for the origin of this sutra, we read: "The Blessed One entered the meditative absorption on the varieties of phenomena called the appearance of the profound." The Buddha is here referred to as the *Bhagavan*, which has been translated in English as the "Blessed One." The Sanskrit term *Bhagavan* connotes someone who has conquered all forces of negativity, that is, the four obstructive forces, or *maras*: the maras of afflictions, of aggregates, of death, and attachment to sensory gratification (Skt. *devaputra*, literally, "divine youth").

The Bhagavan has totally transcended all such obstructive forces and is free from all the effects and limitations caused by these obstructive forces—all the factors obscuring true vision have been removed. We say that the obscurations are removed, rather than that a new kind of vision is attained, because cognition has the natural capacity to understand or to know, and once there are no longer obstructive forces impeding its full function, its natural capacity to know becomes fully apparent. This state of clarity is the all-knowing state, the omniscient mind. In fact, one of the principal characteristics of the Buddha's omniscient mind is that it perceives both the relative and ultimate truths simultaneously within a single cognitive event; whereas, although beings who are not fully awakened may have some insight into the ultimate and relative, they must shift between the two perspectives.

The text then states that the Buddha entered meditative concentration on the varieties of phenomena called "the appearance of the profound." The "profound" here refers to emptiness, which is also often described as "suchness" or as "things just as they are." Emptiness is called "profound" because, to grasp it, one's understanding must penetrate very deeply. This is extremely difficult for the ordinary mind.

ESSENCE AND FORM

The fully enlightened Buddha, who had totally overcome all limitations and negativity and who had actualized all levels of realization, was himself a manifestation of the perfection of wisdom. That perfection of wisdom, the true Dharma, is embodied in the realization of the cessation of suffering and the path that leads to that cessation.

Since we venerate and admire the fruit of the Dharma—the resultant state of full enlightenment—we should also venerate and admire all the causes and conditions that give rise to that state. Such circumstances can be profound and transcendental, such as the three perfect conditions mentioned above, or simple and mundane, such as the fact that when the Buddha taught the Perfection of Wisdom sutras, he arranged the seat upon which he sat to give the teaching. Similarly, in the scriptures we find that often when the Buddha was going to give a teaching, the members of the monastic community would fold their yellow garments and stack them on top of each other to make a throne upon which the Buddha would sit. Such veneration, however, is not accorded to the person himself because of his own greatness, but rather is accorded to the teaching that the teacher embodies and exemplifies. Understanding this point is critical.

In the Tibetan tradition, when someone is giving a teaching, it is often traditional for the teacher to sit on a throne. However, this does not mean that the person sitting on the throne is holy or precious, but rather that the teaching that is being given is to be admired and venerated. To indicate this, it is customary for the teacher to make three prostrations before sitting on the throne. Once the teacher has climbed onto the throne, he or she recites a few verses from a sutra reflecting upon the transient nature of all phenomena. This custom has two main functions: one is to remind the teacher and all present that it is the teaching to which one must pay reverence, and the other is to counter any sense of personal pride that may arise when a teacher sits on a high throne to give a lecture. Furthermore, the throne and the ritual surrounding it serve to remind the teacher to rise above the defilements of mundane motivations for teaching.

The danger of pride is very real. In Tibet, unfortunately, there was sometimes competition among lamas to have the highest throne. There is even a Tibetan expression that speaks of a "throne syndrome"! We read in the Fifth Dalai Lama's autobiography that during his teachings, the organizers of the teaching, being aware of this syndrome, would arrange the thrones of the lamas in attendance to be of equal height. However, some clever attendants of the lamas would manage to slip slates under the cushions on some of the thrones, so although the two thrones themselves were exactly the same height, certain lamas would nonetheless be more highly elevated than others. Ignorant of the true significance of the Dharma, some people would judge the level of spiritual realization of lamas according to such foolish criteria. In addition to judging the importance of lamas in terms of the height of their thrones, people would also judge them in terms of how many horses were in their caravan, concluding that because he had so many horses, a certain teacher must be a lama of great attainment—despite the fact that people also knew perfectly well that a successful bandit could also have many horses in his caravan!

Obviously, the proper way of judging the quality of a lama must be based upon his or her spiritual knowledge, practice, and realization, not on external factors. If one looks at the history of Buddhism in Tibet, there were great spiritual teachers, such as Milarepa, who owned nothing and looked like a beggar, and the Kadampa master Dromtönpa, who was a great teacher yet remained an ordinary, humble nomad. In the twentieth century, we see teachers like the Dzogchen master Dza Patrul Rinpoche, who, in his external appearance, looked completely unremarkable, like an itinerant wanderer. These truly great spiritual teachers carried no external signs of grandeur.

The emphasis placed in Tibet upon the hats that lamas wear is another example of affording respect to a teacher for the wrong reasons. You may have heard of the so-called yellow-hat or red-hat sects. If we look at the example of our original teacher, Buddha Shakyamuni, he, of course, wore no hats at all. And, although the Indian Buddhist masters such as Nagarjuna and Asanga are often depicted wearing hats in Tibetan *tangka* paintings, this may not be historically accurate. In Tibet there is a sensible reason for wearing hats: it is cold! Especially if a teacher is bald, of course, a hat proves very useful. However, Tibetans went to an extreme, making hats of elaborate shapes and sizes to the point where a tendency developed whereby different schools can be distinguished on the basis of their hats. This, I think, is unfortunate.

It is extremely important for us to adopt the essence of the Buddha's teachings and to understand the teachings of the great Indian masters, such as those of Nalanda Monastery. The true gauge by which to evaluate the validity of any teaching should be whether or not it is true Dharma that serves to liberate us from suffering. If the philosophical views, ethical conduct, and meditative practices of a teacher are in keeping with the teachings of Buddha Shakyamuni and the Indian masters, that is what is most important. Although external rituals, such as beating drums, playing cymbals, wearing elaborate costumes, and performing masked dances, have a place in the overall spiritual life, we must know what is of the highest significance.

This is especially important today as Buddhism comes to the West. If we lose track of the true significance of the teachings, there is a danger that Western students of Buddhism will adopt the wrong aspects of Tibetan Buddhist culture—external forms and accessories rather than the inner truth. Unfortunately there are some indications that this may be happening already, with certain people who present themselves as teachers wearing bizarre costumes.

Let me give another example. When I was recently visiting Germany, my hosts had arranged for a tangka to be displayed in my hotel room. It was a tangka of Avalokiteshvara, and below Avalokiteshvara was the small figure of a monk. Of course, it would have been appropriate in a tangka of Avalokiteshvara to have a monk below if the monk were, say, making a mandala offering to Avalokiteshvara, or depicted in meditative posture in the corner. This, however, was not the case: the monk was beating a drum and a cymbal, and next to the monk was the figure of a layperson holding a ritual beverage pot used to make *serkyem* offerings to protector deities. This is utterly inappropriate, because protector deities are propitiated in Tibet often for worldly aspirations rather than spiritual ones. I found out later that the artist was a Westerner. The artist may have been imitating outer forms in what he imagined was a "Tibetan Buddhist" manner, or perhaps he imagined Avalokiteshvara to be some kind of mundane protector, but he clearly did not grasp the significance behind the forms.

This kind of wrongly placed emphasis is by no means endemic to Westerners. For example, if one walks into a typical temple in a Tibetan monastery, there will be an image of Buddha Shakyamuni in the center of the hall, which is as it should be. For Buddhist practitioners, Buddha Shakyamuni is our teacher and guide, the one who reveals to us the path to enlightenment. Therefore, we should entrust, if we can, our entire spiritual well-being to Buddha Shakyamuni. If we need to have some sense of fear, for instance of the consequences of our negative actions, the fear should come out of reverence for the Buddha and his teachings on karma. However, this is often not the case. In such temples, people may briefly pay homage to the Buddha and touch the image with their heads—but they pay more attention to the corner of the temple, where there is a small, dark room, called the protector's shrine room. Each monastery has its own protector, which is depicted in wrathful aspect. When Tibetans walk into this room, they whisper with a sense of awe and may even act terrified of the protector. If they make any offerings, they usually make it to the protector, rather than to the Buddha in the main hall.

In the protector shrine, there is usually a monk in charge of making the ritual beverage offerings, which include tea and alcohol. I heard from someone that in Tibet there was once a monk in one of these protector shrine rooms whose main task was to continually perform this ritual of pouring the offering beverage. Originally bald, the monk found after some time that hair started growing on his head. Someone asked him, "How come you now have hair?" and the monk responded, "I'm not sure, but each time I make the beverage offering, I wipe the leftover drops from my hand onto my head." So for those bald people who would like to grow hair, perhaps this is the solution!

It is important for all of us—including myself—who consider ourselves followers of the Buddha, to constantly check ourselves, to check our motivations, and to maintain our aspiration to liberate all beings from suffering. This is a particular challenge to me in my role as both secular and religious leader of the Tibetan people. Although the practice of merging secular and religious power has sometimes benefited Tibet in the past, shortcomings to this system have led to a great deal of misconduct and suffering. Even in my own case, although I rarely experience a sense of pride when I sit on a high throne to give a teaching, nonetheless, if I leave my thoughts unchecked, mundane concerns may arise in the corner of my mind. For example, I may become delighted if someone compliments my lecture, and I may feel saddened if someone criticizes it. This is a kind of vulnerability to mundane concerns. In order to ensure that one's Dharma practice truly becomes a practice of Dharma, it is important to make sure that one's state of mind and motivation are not defiled by what the Tibetan masters call the *eight mundane concerns.*[13]

Sitting on a throne and holding political power are extremely seductive, and a teacher can never be too vigilant. We should recall the example of the Buddha, who held no worldly authority, and at the beginning of the *Heart Sutra* simply sat down and entered into meditation.

CHAPTER 7

Entering the Bodhisattva Path

THE BODHISATTVA AVALOKITESHVARA

The text of the *Heart Sutra* goes on to read:

> At that time as well, the noble Avalokiteshvara, the bodhi-
> sattva, the great being, clearly beheld the practice of the pro-
> found perfection of wisdom itself and saw that even the
> five aggregates are empty of intrinsic existence.

The next figure we encounter after the Buddha in this sutra is
the bodhisattva Avalokiteshvara. The term *bodhisattva*, as translated
into Tibetan, is comprised of two terms: *jangchub* (Skt. *bodhi*), meaning "enlightenment," and *sempa* (Skt. *sattva*), meaning "hero" or "a
being." So together this conjunction, *jangchub sempa*, gives the meaning "enlightened hero." In the term *jangchub*—"enlightenment"—
the first syllable, *jang*, refers to the overcoming and elimination of all
obstructive forces, and the second syllable, *chub*, signifies the realization of full knowledge. The second part of the name—*sempa*, or
"heroic being"—refers to the bodhisattva's quality of great compassion. It is said that bodhisattvas are beings who, out of intense
compassion, never shift their attention away from sentient beings;

they are perpetually concerned for the welfare of all beings, and they dedicate themselves entirely to securing that welfare. Thus the very name *bodhisattva* indicates a being, who, through wisdom, heroically focuses on the attainment of enlightenment out of compassionate concern for all beings. The word itself conveys the key qualities of such an infinitely altruistic being.

Here, the specific bodhisattva mentioned is Avalokiteshvara, known in Tibetan as Chenrezig. The meaning of the name Chenrezig indicates a bodhisattva who, out of great compassion, never shifts his attention away from sentient beings, always gazing at them with a sense of deep concern. He is also called Lokeshvara (Tib. *Jigten Wangchug*), which literally means "the accomplished master of the world." In the context of the *Heart Sutra*, Avalokiteshvara appears in the form of a bodhisattva on the tenth bodhisattva level.[14]

The text then reads, "the great being, clearly beheld the practice of the profound perfection of wisdom itself." This means that Avalokiteshvara beheld *the way to practice* the profound perfection of wisdom. The next line clarifies what this way is, stating, "[He] saw that even the five aggregates are empty of intrinsic existence." This, then, is the meaning of practicing the perfection of wisdom.

Generally speaking, there are said to be three principal kinds of scriptures attributed to the Buddha: those words that are actually spoken by the Buddha himself, those words spoken by a bodhisattva or a disciple on behalf of the Buddha, and those words spoken by disciples or bodhisattvas that were directly inspired by the Buddha. While this preliminary section of the *Heart Sutra* pertaining to the context of the origin of its teaching belongs to the second category, the main body of the text belongs to the third category, as demonstrated in the next passage:

Thereupon, through the Buddha's inspiration, the venerable Shariputra spoke to the noble Avalokiteshvara, the bodhisattva, the great being, and said, "How should any noble son or noble daughter who wishes to engage in the practice of the profound perfection of wisdom train?"

Shariputra was one of the Buddha's two principal disciples, and the one among all Buddha's disciples said to have the clearest understanding of emptiness. Here, however, Shariputra is to be understood as being a highly attained bodhisattva, not simply a disciple. As the text indicates, the Buddha does not actually utter this particular teaching; rather, the Buddha remains meditatively absorbed in the concentration on the varieties of phenomena called the appearance of the profound. But nonetheless it is the Buddha's meditative concentration that inspires Avalokiteshvara and Shariputra to enter into this dialogue, which gives rise to the teaching contained in the *Heart Sutra*. With the introduction of Shariputra's question, the main body of the teaching on the perfection of wisdom begins.

NOBLE SONS AND NOBLE DAUGHTERS

We read in the text that, "the venerable Shariputra spoke to the noble Avalokiteshvara, the bodhisattva, the great being, and said, 'How should any noble son or noble daughter who wishes to engage in the practice of the profound perfection of wisdom train?'" This reference to "noble sons and noble daughters" literally means sons and daughters of the lineage (Tib. *rig*), or of the family, which in general, can be understood to mean someone who has awakened to his or her buddha nature, the innate potential for enlightenment.

Here, however, the implied reference has to do with three types of beings who realize the three types of enlightenment—of a *shravaka* ("listener"), of a *pratyekabuddha* ("solitary realizer"), and of a buddha. Specifically, the implied reference is to someone whose spiritual inclination is toward the bodhisattva's path to buddhahood. One awakens to such an inclination through the cultivation of great compassion.

This passage in the text, then, refers to practitioners who have deep admiration for the spiritual practices as embodied in the six perfections,[15] which are the key trainings of the bodhisattva, whose mind is gripped by the powerful compassion that aspires to liberate all sentient beings from suffering. Such powerful compassion moistens the heart and awakens the inclination to enter the bodhisattva path. The "noble sons and noble daughters" are those who have generated this compassion and awakened this inclination.

The reference in the text to "noble sons and noble daughters" has additional significance that modern practitioners should bear in mind. This phrase clearly indicates that as far as efficacy of the practice of the perfection of wisdom is concerned, there is no difference based on gender. In fact, this is true as well for all key aspects of the Buddhist path. For example, let us examine the Vinaya teachings on ethics and monastic discipline, which are so essential to the continued survival of the Buddhadharma.

It is said that where the Vinaya as embodied in the practice of the three rites is present, the teachings of the Buddha are also present, and where it is absent, the teachings are also absent.[16] If we carefully analyze the ethical teachings, precepts, and practices of monasticism, we will see that opportunities are given to both male and female practitioners equally. In the Vinaya there is a tradition of full ordination for both women and men; and, with regard to the actual precepts each takes, there is no understanding that one set of precepts is higher than the other. Although, because of the cultural biases of ancient India, fully ordained men, or *bhikshus*, were considered senior to fully ordained women, *bhikshunis*—but there is no hierarchical difference between the vows themselves.

I feel that since there is no discrimination based on gender in the actual teachings, the aspects of the Vinaya that do reflect the gender bias of a given society and time need to be examined carefully, and possibly reconsidered. There may be areas where reforms and modifications are necessary. For example, in the Tibetan monastic tradition, we follow what is called the *Mulasarvastivada* Vinaya tradition, according to which a full-ordination ceremony for women can only be conducted through a gathering of both fully ordained men and fully ordained women. Now it just so happens that the order of fully ordained women in this Vinaya tradition has become extinct; and, since the existence of ordained women in this tradition is a necessary condition for ordaining women in this tradition, this fact effectively meant that it was not possible for women to receive full ordination in the Vinaya tradition we follow in Tibetan Buddhism.[17]

Although I am sympathetic to those who would correct these inequities, changes to the Vinaya can only be made collectively by discussion and consensus; this is not a matter that can be decided by a single individual. Furthermore, since Vinaya practice is common to many Buddhist denominations, such as Theravadin, Tibetan, and Chinese, the issue of modifying the practices needs to be discussed across traditions. Once the members of the various traditions have undertaken a thorough study of their own traditions to determine what the general rules and exceptions are, we can then collectively examine how best to respond to the changing times and cultural contexts. This is a question that requires serious thought.

Buddha Nature

Earlier we noted that the expression "noble son or noble daughter" refers to an individual whose spiritual inclination toward the bodhi-sattva path has been awakened. The word *nature* (*gotra* in Sanskrit) is used differently in the Mahayana and non-Mahayana texts. In the non-Mahayana texts, *gotra* can refer to inclinations that are conducive to spiritual practice, such as having modest desires and the capacity for contentment. Mahayana texts, on the other hand, use *gotra* to refer to one's true nature, also called one's *buddha nature*.

Within the Mahayana, the term *buddha nature* has different shades of meaning. In the Mind-only School, *buddha nature* refers to our fundamental uncontaminated mind that, when untapped, is said to be our "naturally abiding" buddha nature, and when awakened is said to be our "transformed" buddha nature. This naturally abiding buddha nature is known also as *natural nirvana*, or natural liberation, for it exists naturally in all of us. It is because of the presence of this natural nirvana that the pollutants obscuring its expression are said to be separable from the essential nature of the mind, making enlightenment possible. In the Middle Way School, buddha nature is defined differently: it is defined in terms of emptiness, specifically, the mind's emptiness of intrinsic existence. This is also called the clear-light nature of the mind.

THE WAY THINGS ARE

Following the question from Shariputra to Avalokiteshvara, we read
a section connecting the question to the next answer:

> When this had been said, the holy Avalokiteshvara,
> the bodhisattva, the great being, spoke to the ven-
> erable Shariputra and said, "Shariputra, any noble
> son or noble daughter who so wishes to engage in
> the practice of the profound perfection of wisdom
> should clearly see this way: they should see per-
> fectly that even the five aggregates are empty of
> intrinsic existence."

From this point on, the text presents Avalokiteshvara's response
to Shariputra's question, first in a concise summary, then in greater
elaboration. I will explain the meaning of these sections of the *Heart
Sutra* in terms of the explicit subject matter, which is the teaching on
emptiness. And later, in the discussion of the Heart of Wisdom
mantra, I will explain the implicit subject matter, which is the stages
of the path associated with the wisdom of emptiness.

Avalokiteshvara's concise response is that the noble sons and
noble daughters should see insightfully, correctly, and repeatedly,
that "even the five aggregates are empty of intrinsic existence." The
term "even" implies that a comprehensive list of phenomena will be
included in this presentation of emptiness. The five aggregates
(known in Sanskrit as *skandha*) are the physical and mental elements
that together constitute the existence of an individual. Since the five
aggregates are devoid of intrinsic existence, so too is the individual

being constituted by those aggregates. And since the "I," the individual, is devoid of intrinsic existence, devoid of self, so too are all things that are "mine" devoid of intrinsic existence. In other words, not only does the individual—the "appropriator" of physical and mental aggregates—lack intrinsic existence, all the physical and mental aggregates—the "appropriated"—also lack intrinsic existence.

When viewed in this way, all composite phenomena are found to be devoid of intrinsic existence. Since all composite phenomena are empty of intrinsic existence, all non-composite phenomena are empty of intrinsic existence as well. Also, just as sentient beings who are caught in samsaric existence are devoid of intrinsic existence, so too are all the buddhas devoid of intrinsic existence. Finally, and this is a crucial point, even emptiness itself is devoid of intrinsic existence.

As we go through this process of negation, it may seem we are in danger of arriving at the specious conclusion that nothing exits. But, if we understand the meaning of emptiness clearly, as I hope we will begin to, we'll see that this is not what is meant. This clear understanding is subtle, and its precise meaning is debated among different Buddhist schools. While all Buddhist schools reject any notion of *atman,* or inherent self, some accept *anatman,* no-self, only in relation to individual persons, and not in relation to other phenomena. Among schools that do apply no-self to other phenomena, there are different interpretations as well. Some apply no-self to phenomena selectively, while others apply it uniformly to all phenomena. Then, among those who apply the notion uniformly, some deny inherent existence even on a conventional level, while others adhere to certain conventional notions of intrinsic reality.

Predictably, extensive debate arose around these different perspectives, some of which we will touch upon later. The main point I want to underline here is that Avalokiteshvara's telling Shariputra to view the five aggregates as empty of inherent existence is not the same as asserting that they are nonexistent.

CHAPTER 8

Selflessness in Context

ULTIMATE BODHICHITTA

LET US RETURN for a moment to the beginning of this sutra where the Buddha enters into the meditative absorption called "appearance of the profound" and Avalokiteshvara beholds the practice of the profound perfection of wisdom. Generally speaking, the expression "appearance of the profound" refers to the bodhisattva deeds, which are encompassed in the practice of the six perfections. Here, however, the expression refers particularly to the perfection of wisdom, known in Sanskrit as *prajnaparamita*. What the text means by "perfection of wisdom" is a direct, unmediated realization of emptiness that is also called "ultimate bodhichitta." This is not the direct realization of emptiness alone; rather it is this direct realization *in union with bodhichitta*—the aspiration to become a buddha in order to free all beings. This union of wisdom and method constitutes the first *bhumi*, or level of bodhisattva attainment.

The importance of this altruistic aspiration cannot be overstated. Bodhichitta is not only important as a motivating factor at the beginning of practice, it is also important as a complementary and a reinforcing factor during every stage of the path. The bodhichitta aspiration is twofold, comprised both of the wish to help others and of the wish to become enlightened so that one's assistance will be supremely effective.

THE DOCTRINE OF NO-SELF

Earlier, in Avalokiteshvara's concise summary of the presentation of emptiness, we read that someone who wishes to engage in the practice of the perfection of wisdom "should clearly see this way: they should see perfectly that even the five aggregates are empty of intrinsic existence." As we saw in the previous chapter, the concept of the five aggregates is intimately connected with the issue of the nature and existence of the self, the topic to which we now turn our attention. There evolved many philosophical schools in ancient India that contemplated this question in depth, all of which underlined the critical importance of this question, particularly in relation to our understanding of causality.

As I often state, we all naturally possess an innate desire to be happy and overcome suffering. But how exactly does suffering arise? How exactly does happiness arise? What is the nature of the self that experiences suffering and happiness? When we try to understand the causal processes that underlie suffering and happiness, one realizes that suffering and happiness arise on the basis of multiple conditions. These conditions include internal factors, such as our sense organs, experiences, perceptions, as well as external factors, such as forms, sounds, smells, tastes, and tactile objects. This leads us to inquire, What exactly is the nature of these things that give rise to our experience of pain and pleasure? Do they really exist and, if so, in what way?

The Indian philosophical traditions, both Buddhist and

non-Buddhist, have presented various philosophical answers to questions concerning the origin of both the internal and external worlds, and the nature of the subject that undergoes those experiences. Some schools of thought maintain that things and events—including the self—come into being with no cause, while others argue that there is an absolute, original cause that is eternal, unchanging, and unitary. All of these questions hinge, in one way or another, on an understanding of the self. So let's take some time to examine certain aspects of our understanding of the self.

We may think that the self is identical with the body. For example, if there is pain in one's hand, one has the instinctive thought, "*I am in pain.*" Although one's hand is not oneself, one instinctively identifies with that experience and, in this way, the sense of self arises naturally in relation to the body.

At the same time, however, the sense of "me" is not completely identifiable with the body. Consider the following thought experiment: If someone were to offer us the opportunity to exchange our old, infirm body for a more youthful, healthy body, we would most likely be willing, from the very depths of our heart, to make this exchange. This suggests that we believe, at least on some level, that there is someone, some non-bodily self, who would benefit from this exchange of bodies.

We can extend this thought experiment into the mental realm by considering how we would respond if we were given the opportunity to exchange our ignorant, deluded mind for the Buddha's fully enlightened mind. Surely we would be willing to enter into this exchange, imagining again that there is someone, some non-mental self, who would benefit. This suggests that we identify the self neither entirely with the body nor entirely with the mind.

In our naïve view of the world, we cling to our feeling that there is a self that, in some sense, is the master of our body and mind—an agent that is independent and bears its own distinct identity. Those who believe in rebirth may imagine that it is this self that spans across successive lives of the same individual. Even in the case of someone who does not believe in multiple lives, there is a notion of a somehow unchanging entity, a "me," that goes through different stages of life, from childhood to middle age and so on to old age and death. Clearly, we have a belief that there is something, in many lives or in one life, that retains continuity over time.

It is this sense of continuity that leads people in many non-Buddhist religions to assert an eternal soul, or *atman*, that is unitary, unchanging, and independent of the physical and mental constituents of the person—in other words, an absolute reality. However, the Buddhist schools teach that if one searches for the essence of this self, this absolute reality, with sufficient rigor and sufficiently critical analysis, one will inevitably discover it cannot be found.

This kind of search reveals that it is only on the basis of the physical and mental aggregates of the individual that one can speak of the continuity of the person. So, for instance, when an individual's body and mind age (the aggregates), one can say that the person ages. Buddhists, therefore, reject the notion of an eternal, unchanging principle, and further argue that the conception of self as possessing such characteristics is a completely metaphysical construct, a mental fabrication. Although all beings have an innate *sense* of self, the *concept* of an eternal, unchanging, unitary, and autonomous self is present only in the minds of those who have thought about the issue. After their own critical investigation, however, Buddhists conclude that the self can be understood only as a dependent phenomenon contingent upon the physical and mental aggregates.

In addition to negating the concept of an eternal and absolute self, Buddhists also deny the naïve sense of self as master of the body and mind. Since Buddhists claim you cannot find any self beyond the physical and mental components, this precludes the possibility of an independent agent controlling them. From the Buddhist point of view, the non-Buddhist conception of self as an absolute, eternal principle reinforces the mistaken instinct to believe in a self that controls our body and mind. Therefore (with the exception of some subdivisions of the Vaibhashika School) all classical Indian Buddhist schools reject the concept of a substantially real, enduring eternal principle called "self."

THE FOUR SEALS

We have established then that the doctrine of no-self is central to Buddhism. In fact, there are four such central axioms that characterize the Buddhist understanding of existence. The four axioms, also known as the *four seals*, are:

All composite phenomena are impermanent;
All contaminated phenomena are unsatisfactory;
All phenomena are empty and devoid of self-existence; and
Nirvana is true peace.

Let's examine each of these in turn.

All composite phenomena are impermanent

The first axiom states that all the things and events we experience go through a perpetual process of change and disintegration even on a moment-by-moment basis. All things come into being at a certain point and also cease to exist at a certain point—they break, disintegrate, or perish, and so on. This is something that we all can observe in our day-to-day experience with our possessions, our physical ailments, and our emotional states. We do not require any particular logical proof to arrive at this understanding in a general way. However, for something to come into being and then later to cease, the process of change must be occurring continuously, moment by moment. The cessation of any phenomenon does not come about instantaneously, but as a result of an ongoing process.

It is extremely difficult, if not impossible, to understand how things suddenly come to an end without recognizing this process of moment-to-moment disintegration. The fact that things do indeed eventually come to an end suggests that they are necessarily undergoing moment-to-moment change. Virtually all Buddhist schools accept that all things and events carry in themselves the seed of their own cessation from the very moment they come into being. It is not the case that only through the effects of some other object or event does a given object or event cease to be; it contains the seed for its cessation within itself.

An example may clarify this point: Consider a building, such as a house. Our ordinary understanding of causality would lead us to say that the house ceases only because someone demolishes it. However, the fact that all composite phenomena, in this case a house, are impermanent leads us to understand that the house will eventually cease whether we demolish it or not. The house is continuously decaying in myriad ways and will ultimately cease because it is, by its very nature, impermanent.

So according to Buddhism, it is not the case, as we tend to believe in our naïve understanding of the world, that one event causes something, and another condition at some later point brings about the thing's cessation. In other words, Buddhism does not accept that things first come into being, remain in an unchanging state for a period of time, and then suddenly cease to exist.

Nevertheless, when we conceive the origination of things or events, we tend to view them from an affirmative perspective—a thing comes into existence, perhaps by being born, and persists, perhaps by growing. In contrast, when we think of something coming to an end, going out of existence, we tend to conceive this in negative terms—the cessation of something that really existed previously. We see these two—origination and cessation—as contradictory and incompatible; we imagine they are two mutually exclusive states of being.

However, this first axiom of Buddhism tells us that, because phenomena are impermanent, they continually, moment by moment, undergo a process of change. This "momentariness," then, is the Buddhist definition of impermanence. When we understand impermanence in these terms, we will see that, in fact, origination and cessation are not mutually exclusive. They are instead one phenomenon—namely, impermanence—viewed from two perspectives.

The very fact that something comes into being makes it possible, and indeed necessary, for that thing to cease. Its origination is the primary condition for its ultimate cessation. So when we understand the impermanence of all things, we understand that they are going through this process of cessation in each moment. This is the significance of the first axiom of Buddhism, that all composite phenomena are impermanent.

All contaminated phenomena are unsatisfactory

The second axiom states that all contaminated things and events are unsatisfactory, meaning that they are all in the nature of suffering. As we saw in chapter 3, there are three levels of suffering. The suffering referred to by this axiom is the third level, the pervasive suffering that is the very nature of our conditioned existence. It is pervasive since all our actions are currently performed in ignorance of the true nature of phenomena, and therefore the results of these actions, our experiences, are all caused by, and remain under the domination of, karma and mental afflictions. "Contaminated" here simply describes products of karma and mental afflictions.

Here, it may be helpful to reflect on a few passages from the scriptures. In the *Sutra on the Ten Grounds (Dasabhumi Sutra)*, the Buddha makes the following statement:

This entire world of three realms is nothing but the mind.

The Mind-only School of Buddhism interprets this passage to mean that the external, material world that we perceive is nothing but an illusion—a projection of our mind. However, others understand this statement very differently. For example, in interpreting this statement from the sutra, Chandrakirti writes the following in his *Supplement to the Middle Way (Madhyamakavatara)*:

Failing to see "person" and so on—
which are asserted by the *tirthikas*

in their own treatises—as being the creator,
the conqueror taught that mind alone is the creator.[18]

Chandrakirti understands the Buddha's statement that the entire
world—the natural environment and the beings within it—is created by the mind to be a rejection of the concept of an independent, absolute, divine creator. Even so, there is still a sense in which
Chandrakirti's own Middle Way School does accept that the entire
universe is created by the mind.

How should we understand this idea? If we trace the origin of
our present physical body, we can follow its material continuum
back to the beginning of the universe. That is to say, we can discern,
through modern science, that the matter that comprises our bodies
all originated with the Big Bang. But from the perspective of traditional Buddhist cosmology, the continuum of our material body
extends even beyond the beginning of the material universe to a
time when the universe was empty and remained in the state of what
the *Kalachakra Tantra* refers to as "space particles." These space particles are not absolute or fixed but are rather subject, like all matter,
to the laws of impermanence and change.

If we look at the purely material level of atoms or particles, we
can ask, "What is it, in the process of the evolution of the physical universe through the aggregation of particles and atoms, that
caused the universe to become directly relevant to sentient beings'
experience of suffering and happiness?" From the Buddhist point of
view, this is where karma enters into the picture. *Karma* refers to
actions undertaken with intention. And given that the entire development of our unenlightened existence is a consequence of our
undisciplined state of mind, in the final analysis, the mind is the

creator of our entire existence. Karma is what fuels the whole evolution of an individual's existence in samsara.

Although there are physical and verbal karmic actions, karma is primarily a mental event. Karmic acts are motivated by and rooted in the mental afflictions, which in turn are rooted in fundamental ignorance, namely, the erroneous belief in an enduring self-existence of things. Furthermore, it is an aspect of the law of causality that the character of the effects must correspond to the character of the causes.[19] Consequently, all experiences and events caused by an undisciplined state of mind—that is, as a result of karmic actions and mental afflictions—are, in the final analysis, contaminated. An action, such as making offerings to the Buddha, may conventionally be positive, but until we have overcome ignorance through the direct realization of emptiness, that action is still contaminated and in the nature of suffering.

There is an intimate relationship of inference between these first two axioms of Buddhism—that all composite phenomena are impermanent and that all contaminated phenomena are unsatisfactory; we can infer the second axiom from the first. The statement in the first axiom that all composite phenomena are impermanent implies that as long as a thing is a product of other causes and conditions, then it is under the control of factors other than itself. In the case of contaminated phenomena in the second axiom, the implication is that they are products of, and therefore under the power of, mental afflictions, which arise out of our fundamental ignorance. The first axiom explains causality, while the second explains the causal process of unenlightened existence.

All phenomena are empty and devoid of self-existence

This third axiom states that all phenomena—all things and events—lack intrinsic reality. This is the traditional phrasing of the Buddhist assertion of emptiness, which we have been examining at length throughout this book, and which plays such a key role in understanding the *Heart Sutra*.

Let's briefly review our previous discussion here: All phenomena, including the self, lack intrinsic existence; however, because of our fundamental ignorance, we ascribe intrinsic existence to them. This fundamental ignorance is thus not a state of mere *unknowing*; rather it is an active state of *mis-knowing*. In our state of mis-knowing, we mistakenly perceive things contrary to the way they really are. The more one uncovers the truth about the nature of reality, the weaker the force of this ignorance becomes, and, as the nature of reality becomes more apparent, the realization that this ignorance is erroneous will become stronger.

Nirvana is true peace

Once we deeply ascertain the distorted nature of our mistaken perspective within meditation, its dominion over us will begin to diminish gradually and naturally. As this happens, we become able to envision the possibility of gaining *total* freedom from such erroneous beliefs. Such freedom—complete liberation from the ignorance that grasps onto the self-existence of things—is the only true, lasting state of happiness and spiritual freedom, the only true peace, the only true liberation.

CHAPTER 9

Interpreting Emptiness

THE TWO TYPES OF SELFLESSNESS

BEFORE WE RETURN to examining the text of the *Heart Sutra*, let's look at selflessness through the eyes of the various Buddhist schools so that we can attain a more refined understanding of emptiness as presented in the *Heart Sutra*. As I explained earlier, a belief in "selflessness" is essential to all Buddhist schools, but there is a variety of interpretations among them as to what precisely that term means. Within the Tibetan monastic curriculum, there is an entire genre of literature outlining in detail each school's way of understanding these matters; these are known as the tenets (*druptha* in Tibetan) of each particular school. Within this literature, the various philosophical perspectives are ascribed to four main schools prevalent in ancient India, and the presentation of selflessness becomes progressively subtler with the arising of each school. These schools are the *Vaibhashika* School, the *Sautrantika* School, the *Chittamatra* (Mind-only) School, and the *Madhyamaka* (Middle Way) School.

Tibetan Buddhists generally subscribe to the views of the final school, the Middle Way School. You might wonder why it is, then, that so much time should be spent dissecting the views of these other schools. How does it relate to the larger enterprise of liberation and enlightenment? Since the correct understanding of emptiness is crucial for success in eliminating the mental afflictions, it is important to examine the many places where we might stray from the path of right understanding. The views of earlier schools represent ways that Buddhists have historically fallen short of the most exhaustive application of the Buddha's teachings on emptiness. Studying the tenets of these schools helps us avoid becoming stuck in what is only a partial understanding of the true nature of emptiness. It also gives us a greater appreciation for the profundity of the most subtle standpoint. Of course a correct intellectual view is no substitute for the direct realization of emptiness, which is nonconceptual, but it is a vital tool nonetheless in the task of approaching that realization.

The texts on tenets differentiate between two kinds of selflessness: *selflessness of the person* and *selflessness of phenomena.* "Person" here refers to our strong sense of self, the "I" with which we refer to ourselves. "Phenomena" refers primarily to the mental and physical aggregates of the person, but includes all other phenomena as well. Among the four Buddhist schools, the two earlier ones—the Vaibhashika School and the Sautrantika School—speak only of the importance of meditating on the selflessness of the person, and do not accept any notion of the selflessness of phenomena. However, the two latter schools—the Mind-only School and the Middle Way School—accept the doctrines of both the selflessness of the person and of phenomena. These schools would argue that a limited notion of selflessness, one referring only to the person, prevents us from eliminating the full range of obscurations and afflictions, as we shall see below. So, although firmly realizing emptiness of person alone would be a tremendous accomplishment, it still falls short of complete liberation from suffering.

THE MIND-ONLY INTERPRETATION

On the whole, we naturally tend to trust our everyday perceptions; we assume their validity without it even occurring to us to question them. We naïvely believe that the way we perceive things is identical with the way things are. And so, because events and things, including the self, appear to have objective reality, we conclude, tacitly and often without any reflection at all, that they do in fact have an objective reality. Only through the process of careful analysis can we see that this is not so, that our perceptions do not accurately reflect objective reality.

As we have discussed earlier, all sensory experiences of the external world arise through the coalescence of three factors: a sensory faculty, an object, and our mental perception. This perception of an external object then gives rise to a subjective evaluation: we find the object either attractive or unattractive. We then project desirability or undesirability onto the object, feeling the quality to be an objective reality inherent in the object. On the basis of this projection, we may then develop a strong emotional reaction. If the object is seen as undesirable, we feel distaste or revulsion; and if the object is seen as desirable, we feel attachment or desire. But, as we have seen, there is nothing intrinsically real in the object that qualifies it to have the label "attractive." The quality of attractiveness that we perceive is, to a large extent, purely subjective. It is particularly useful to examine our experience in the wake of a strong emotional response, since this kind of experience brings our sense of self sharply and immediately into focus.

In the Mind-only view, what is seen as objectively real and existing "out there," the object, is nothing more than a projection of our mind, the subject. Thus, subject and object are seen as ultimately non-dual. From a practical perspective, this view is very useful: it is not hard to see how recognizing that the qualities we perceive in objects are merely aspects of our own mind could have a dramatic impact on reducing our attachment to those external objects.

So, although the Mind-only School rejects the reality of a self and rejects the reality of an external, objective material reality, it nonetheless maintains that subjective *experience*—that is to say, the mind—does have substantial reality. Followers of the Mind-only School assert that if the mind did not possess an intrinsic, substantial reality, there would be no basis upon which to make meaningful distinctions between good and evil, between what is harmful and what is beneficial. They assume that, for a phenomenon to exist, it has to have an objective, substantial basis upon which to posit its various functions.

And yet, in the Mind-only view, all things and events are not *purely* mental constructs. If that were the case, white could become black and black could become white merely by our thinking them so. Since this is not the case, one must therefore accept, this view goes on to assert, that the inner subjective experience, the world of consciousness, also has substantial reality. Consequently, for the Mind-only School, the explanations of emptiness found in the Perfection of Wisdom sutras cannot be taken at face value. They argue that if we were to take statements like "there is no form, no feeling, no discriminations," literally, this would constitute falling into the mistaken extreme of nihilism, which contradicts the law of cause and effect.

The Mind-only understanding of the Buddha's teaching on emptiness in the Perfection of Wisdom sutras is primarily based on a particular set of assertions in the *Sutra Unraveling the Thought of the*

Buddha (Samdhinirmochanasutra), in which a theory called the "three natures" is presented in great detail. According to this assertion, all things and events possess three principal natures. *Dependent nature,* that is, the interplay of various specific causes and conditions, is said to be the *basis* of a phenomenon's existence. Upon the basis of this dependent nature, we project an independent reality onto the phenomenon; this *imputed nature* is what appears to us as real. Finally, the *ultimate nature* of a phenomenon is the negation of this imputation, namely, the phenomenon's emptiness.

Since all things and events are said to possess these three natures, the Mind-only School argues that "devoid of intrinsic, or self, nature" in the Perfection of Wisdom sutras means different things in relation to each of these natures. They argue that dependent phenomena are devoid of intrinsic nature in that they lack *independent origination*—that is, they do not come into being from themselves. Imputed phenomena are devoid of intrinsic nature in that they lack *intrinsic characteristics*—that is, the various characteristics we perceive in a phenomenon are a function of our mind. Finally, ultimate phenomena are devoid of intrinsic nature in that they do not abide as absolutes—which is to say, even emptiness has no absolute, objective reality. The Mind-only School interprets the meaning of the Perfection of Wisdom sutras in the context of their doctrine of these three natures.

In consequence, the Mind-only School divides the Buddha's scriptures into those that are *definitive*, which can be accepted literally, and those that are *provisional*, which cannot be accepted literally and require interpretation to be fully grasped. A teaching that withstands the scrutiny of critical evaluation, at least as followers of the Mind-only school conduct it, is taken definitively, whereas a teaching that contradicts their conception of the Buddha's ultimate intention is said to require interpretation.

One important subdivision of the Mind-only School is the "followers of scripture." While rejecting the notion of an eternal self, this branch of the Mind-only School posits something called the foundational consciousness (*alaya vijnana*) to be the real person or the basis of self. The original proponent of this school felt that, if the person or self is identified with the gross mental consciousness, it would be difficult to posit the existence of the person at certain times; for example, when a person faints or is in deep sleep, or when a meditator attains states that are totally devoid of conscious activity. The foundational consciousness provides the Mind-only School with a more stable faculty for positing the identity of the person. In addition, the foundational consciousness serves as the repository for the four propensities[20] and is where the imprints of all our karmic actions are stored. The deluded thought "I am" that arises on the basis of this foundational consciousness is sometimes separated out as the "deluded consciousness." Thus one proponent of this branch of the Mind-only School posits eight classes of consciousness—the five sensory consciousnesses, gross mental consciousness, foundational consciousness, and deluded consciousness.

DEFINITIVE VERSUS PROVISIONAL INTERPRETATIONS

Earlier we observed that one of the principal features of the Buddha's teachings is that they were spoken to accord with the varying spiritual and mental needs and dispositions of the listeners. The tenets of the various schools can similarly be viewed as fulfilling these diverse needs. We have just seen how the Mind-only School distinguishes definitive from provisional teachings, and in fact each school has its own criteria for determining whether a teaching of the Buddha is definitive or provisional. In each case, the process is similar: first, one uses analysis to determine the Buddha's ultimate intention in making a particular statement; second, one determines the Buddha's contextual rationale for making a particular statement; and third, one demonstrates the logical inconsistency, if any, that arises when the particular statement is taken literally.

The need for such an approach is found in the Buddha's own sutras. There is a verse in which Buddha urges his followers to take his words as they might accept from a jeweler a metal that appears to be gold: only after seeing that the metal does not tarnish when burned, can be easily cut, and can be polished to a bright shine should the metal be accepted as gold. Thus, the Buddha gives us his permission to critically examine even his own teachings. Buddha suggests we make a thorough inquiry into the truth of his words and verify them for ourselves, and only then "accept them, but not out of reverence."[21]

Taking direction from statements such as these, ancient Indian monastic universities, such as Nalanda, developed a tradition whereby students would critically subject their own teachers' scholastic work to analysis. Such critical analysis was seen in no way to go against the great admiration and reverence the students had for their teachers. The famous Indian master Vasubandhu, for example, had a disciple known as Vimuktisena, who was said to excel Vasubandhu in his understanding of the Perfection of Wisdom sutras. He questioned Vasubandhu's Mind-only interpretation and instead developed his own understanding of the sutras in accord with the Middle Way School.

An example of this in the Tibetan Buddhist tradition is Alak

Damchoe Tsang, who was one of the disciples of the great nineteenth-century Nyingma master Ju Mipham. Although Alak Damchoe Tsang had tremendous admiration and reverence for his teacher, he voiced his objections to some of Mipham's writings. Once a student of Alak Damchoe Tsang is said to have asked if it was appropriate to critically object to the writings of his own teacher. Alak Damchoe Tsang's immediate response was, "If one's great teacher says things that are not correct, one must take even one's lama to task!"

There is a Tibetan saying, "Retain your reverence and admiration for the person, but subject the writing to thorough critical analysis." This demonstrates a healthy attitude and illustrates the Buddhist tradition known as the approach of the *four reliances:*

Do not rely merely on the person, but on the words;
Do not rely merely on the words, but on their meaning;
Do not rely merely on the provisional meaning, but on
    the definitive meaning; and
Do not rely merely on intellectual understanding, but on
    direct experience.

The Middle Way Interpretation

In contrast to the Mind-only School, the Middle Way School reads the Perfection of Wisdom sutras as definitive, accepting the statement that "all things and events are devoid of any intrinsic existence" as literal. The Middle Way view does not discriminate between the existential status of subject and object—between mind and world. The *Hundred Thousand Verses on the Perfection of Wisdom* explicitly presents this view with the statement that, on the ultimate level, *all* phenomena do not exist. So, for the Middle Way School, the Perfection of Wisdom sutras remain literal, and the emptiness of all phenomena becomes definitive.

This distinction between the tenets of the Mind-only School and the Middle Way School may not immediately seem important, but if we examine it closely we can appreciate its significance. The Mind-only School acknowledges the emptiness of phenomena in the external world, and because of this they may be able to cut through attachment and aversion to external phenomena by recognizing the emptiness of these phenomena. But this is not enough. Unless one is able to recognize the emptiness of the *internal* world as well, one may become attached to such experiences as tranquility or bliss, and averse to such experiences as sadness or fear. Understanding the emptiness of all phenomena—not discriminating between internal and external, mind and world—is the refinement of the Middle Way school. Understanding this thoroughly for ourselves enables us to break completely free of the bondage of the afflictions in all circumstances.

Some Middle Way proponents, followers of a school known as the Yogachara-Madhyamaka School, maintain the Mind-only distinction between internal and external worlds, but apply the teachings of emptiness equally to both. On the whole, however, the Middle Way schools teach that, when it comes to the ultimate nature of reality, it is just not helpful to discriminate between external and internal worlds.

Furthermore, Madhyamikas argue that one of the premises for the Mind-only rejection of the reality of the external world is their belief that such a reality presupposes the existence of indivisible atoms or particles. Such particles, if they existed, would be the ultimate constitutive matter and act as a basis for the existence of the objective world. Since the notion of an indivisible, absolute atom is untenable for them, they argue that one must reject the objective reality of the material world.

The Madhyamikas respond to this by pointing out that one can use the same argument to negate the substantial reality of the internal world. For, in order to accept the substantial reality of consciousness or mind, one must presuppose the existence of indivisible moments of cognition, which are also ultimate constituents of reality. This they say is untenable, for one can conceive consciousness only on the basis of a continuous, dependently originated stream of cognition, not as discrete moments of consciousness. Thus, even the internal world of consciousness and cognition is devoid of substantial reality. By applying this reasoning nondiscriminately to both the external world of matter and the internal world of consciousness, the adherents of the Middle Way argue that one can undermine the basis for attachment to both the external and internal worlds.

The Two Middle Way Schools

The great Indian master Nagarjuna was the founder of the Middle Way School, and his most famous text is his *Fundamentals of the Middle Way*. Among the many readings of Nagarjuna's text by subsequent Indian masters, those by Buddhapalita, Bhavaviveka, and Chandrakirti were particularly influential. In his commentary, Bhavaviveka criticized some aspects of the earlier reading by Buddhapalita. In defense of Buddhapalita, Chandrakirti wrote the highly influential commentary on *Fundamentals of the Middle Way* called *Clear Words* (*Prasannapada*).

One of the principal differences between Buddhapalita's and Bhavaviveka's interpretations has to do with the notion of "commonly appearing objects." That is, when engaged in a discourse on the ultimate mode of being of things, whether it is possible for two opposing parties to have a shared perception of an object that is equally valid from the perspectives of both parties. Bhavaviveka asserts that this is possible. In asserting an objective reality in some measure independent of the perceiver, Bhavaviveka accepts that a degree of intrinsic existence can be attributed to things and events. For example, Bhavaviveka seems to maintain that although the person or self is a mental construct contingent upon the aggregates, if one searches for the true referent of the term "person," one should be able to find something that is substantially real. Bhavaviveka singles out the mental consciousness as being the true person that can be found under ultimate analysis. Chandrakirti refutes this idea.

Based on these differences, two principal strains of Middle Way philosophy arose. The differences between these groups are reflected in the method used by their followers to establish emptiness. As Nagarjuna does in his *Fundamentals of the Middle Way*, Buddhapalita principally uses a form of reasoning known as consequentialist (*prasanga* in Sanskrit). This *reductio ad absurdum* reasoning proceeds primarily by demonstrating internal inconsistencies in the view of an opponent. In contrast, Bhavaviveka and his followers reason from the basis of established syllogisms. Due to this difference in methodology, these two schools came to be known as the *Svatantrika*, or "autonomous" school, those who accept autonomous syllogisms, and the *Prasangika* school, those who prefer the consequentialist style of proof. Bhavaviveka's Svatantrika school was later upheld by masters such as Jnanagarbha, while Buddhapalita's Prasangika school was upheld by Chandrakirti and Shantideva.

It is clearly evident from reading his commentary on Nagarjuna's *Fundamentals of the Middle Way* that Buddhapalita did not accept the notion of intrinsic existence even conventionally. When commenting on Nagarjuna's opening verse, which negates the four possible types of origination—from itself, from other, from both self and other, and from neither self nor other—Buddhapalita observes that if we subject the process of origination to critical analysis, origination itself cannot be found to exist. However, since things do originate as a result of causes and conditions, he explicitly states that we can understand the notion of origination on a conventional level. He states further that if phenomena possessed an objective, intrinsic nature, it would not be necessary to posit their identity and existence in relation to other factors. This very fact, that things and events can only be understood in relation to, or in dependence upon, other factors, suggests that they do not exist by means of an intrinsic nature.

Bhavaviveka agreed with Buddhapalita that all modes of origination have no *ultimate* intrinsic existence, but he argued that the process of origination of things from factors other than themselves has a *conventional* intrinsic existence. Chandrakirti, defending Buddhapalita's position, explicitly rejects this. In his *Supplement to the Middle Way*, Chandrakirti states that both the subject—the person who experiences pain and pleasure—and the objects of that person are revealed to be unfindable, possessing no objective, independent reality, even on a conventional level. Chandrakirti says that we can understand their existential status by means of understanding their conventional reality, but even that conventional reality itself is empty.

According to Chandrakirti, intrinsic existence is simply false, and its negation constitutes the final understanding of emptiness.

EMPTINESS AND DEPENDENT ORIGINATION

So, for the Prasangikas, "emptiness" means "emptiness of intrinsic existence." It does not mean that nothing exists, but only that things do not possess the intrinsic reality we naïvely thought they did. So we must ask, in what way *do* phenomena exist? In chapter 24 of his *Fundamentals of the Middle Way*, Nagarjuna argues that the existential status of phenomena can only be understood in terms of dependent origination. "Dependence" for some of the lower schools means dependence upon causes and conditions, but for the Prasangikas, dependence primarily means dependence upon the conceptual designation of a subject.

We find support for this view in the sutras. In the *Questions of Anavatapta* we read a passage stating that whatever comes into being in dependence upon other conditions must be devoid of intrinsic origination. The sutra states:

> That which is born from conditions is unborn,
> for it is devoid of intrinsic origination.
> That which depends upon conditions is declared empty.
> One who knows this emptiness remains tranquil.[22]

We find similar passages in Nagarjuna's *Compendium of Sutras (Sutrasamuccaya)* and in Shantideva's *Compendium of Deeds (Shiksasamuccaya)* where, in the chapter on wisdom, Shantideva cites a number of sutras that negate the notion of intrinsic existence in relation to extensive taxonomies of phenomena, like the ones we see in the *Heart Sutra*. Shantideva concludes by pointing out that all the phenomena described in the taxonomies are mere name and designation.

The point here is that, if things and events do not exist at all, it would be impossible to make coherent sense of the enumerations in the *Heart Sutra* of things like the five aggregates and the thirty-seven aspects of the path to enlightenment. If the doctrine of emptiness denied the reality of these phenomena, it would be pointless to enumerate them. This suggests that things exist, but not intrinsically so; existence can only be understood in terms of dependent origination.

If one understands emptiness as described by the Prasangika Madhyamaka School—that each and every phenomenon lacks even a trace of intrinsic existence—there is simply no basis for grasping onto selfhood to arise. From this practical perspective, the Prasangika Madhyamaka's understanding of emptiness constitutes the highest and most subtle understanding of the Buddha's teaching on no-self.

Developing an
Unmistaken View of Reality

CORRECTLY REFUTING INTRINSIC EXISTENCE

ALL OF THE FOREGOING philosophical discussion suggests the following basic point: The way we tend to perceive things to be does not accord with the way they are. Again, this does not nihilistically deny the fact of our experience. The *existence* of things and events is not in dispute; it is the *manner in which* they exist that must be clarified. That is the point of going through these complex analyses.

It is essential that any spiritual aspirant cultivate a perspective that directly opposes the erroneous belief that grasps onto the concrete existence of things and events. Only by cultivating such a view can we begin to diminish the power of the afflictions that dominate us. Any daily practices we engage in—mantra recitation, visualizations, and so on—will by themselves be unable to counter this fundamental ignorance. Simply forming the aspiration "May this deluded grasping at intrinsic existence disappear" is insufficient; we must thoroughly clarify our understanding of the nature of emptiness. That is the only way to be completely free of suffering. Furthermore, without this clear understanding, it is conceivable that, instead of helping us *counter* our grasping at concrete reality, visualizing deities and reciting mantras could even *reinforce* our deluded grasping at the objective reality of the world and the self.

Many Buddhist practices proceed by way of applying an antidote. For example, we cultivate the aspiration to benefit others as an antidote to self-cherishing, and we cultivate our understanding of the impermanent nature of reality as an antidote to seeing things and events as fixed. In the same manner, by cultivating the correct insight into the nature of reality—the emptiness of things and events—we gradually are able to release ourselves from grasping at intrinsic existence and eventually eliminate it.

UNDERSTANDING THE TWO TRUTHS

In the *Heart Sutra*, we read:

> They should see perfectly that even the five aggregates are empty of intrinsic existence. Form is emptiness, emptiness is form; emptiness is not other than form, form too is not other than emptiness.

This passage presents Avalokiteshvara's summary response to Shariputra's question about how to practice the perfection of wisdom. The phrase "empty of intrinsic existence" is Avalokiteshvara's reference to the subtlest, highest understanding of emptiness, the absence of intrinsic existence. Avalokiteshvara elaborates his answer, which begins with the following lines, "Form is emptiness, emptiness is form; emptiness is not other than form, form too is not other than emptiness."

It's important for us to avoid the misapprehension that

emptiness is an absolute reality or an independent truth. Emptiness must be understood as the true nature of things and events. Thus we read, "Form is emptiness, emptiness is form; emptiness is not other than form, form too is not other than emptiness." This does not refer to some kind of Great Emptiness out there somewhere, but to the emptiness of a specific phenomenon, in this case form, or matter.

The statement that "apart from form there is no emptiness" suggests that the emptiness of form is nothing other than the form's ultimate nature. Form lacks intrinsic or independent existence; thus its nature is emptiness. This nature—emptiness—is not independent of form, but rather is a *characteristic of* form; emptiness is form's mode of being. One must understand form and its emptiness in unity; they are not two independent realities.

Let us look more closely at Avalokiteshvara's two statements: that form is emptiness and emptiness is form. The first statement, "form is emptiness," implies that what we recognize as form comes to exist as a result of the aggregation of many causes and conditions, not by its own independent means. Form is a composite phenomenon, composed of many parts. Because it comes into being and continues to exist based on other causes and conditions, it is a dependent phenomenon. This dependence means that form is consequently empty of any intrinsic, self-existent reality, and therefore form is said to be emptiness.

Now let's turn to his next statement, that emptiness is form. Since form lacks independent existence, it can never be isolated from other phenomena. Consequently, dependence suggests a kind of openness and malleability in relation to other things. Because of this fundamental openness, form is not fixed but rather subject to change and causality. In other words, since forms arise from inter-actions of causes and conditions and do not have independent and fixed reality, they lend themselves to the possibility of interaction with other forms and therefore other causes and conditions. All of this is part of a complex, interconnected reality. Because forms have no fixed, isolated identity, we can say that emptiness is the basis for the existence of form. In fact, in some sense, we can even say that emptiness *creates* form. One can then understand the statement that "emptiness is form" in terms of form being a manifestation or expression of emptiness, something that comes out of emptiness.

This seemingly abstract relationship of form and emptiness is somewhat analogous to the relationship of material objects and space. Without empty space, material objects cannot exist; space is the medium for the physical world. This analogy breaks down, how-ever, insofar as material objects can be said, in some sense, to be separate from the physical space they occupy, whereas form and the emptiness of form cannot.

In the *Lankavatara Sutra,* we find descriptions of seven different senses in which something can be said to be empty. For our purposes, let's just examine two manners of being empty. The first manner of being empty is known as "emptiness of other"—in the way that a temple may be empty of monks. Here, the emptiness (of the temple) is separate from what is being negated (the presence of monks).

In contrast, when we say "form is emptiness," we are negating an intrinsic essence of form. This manner of being empty is called *emptiness of intrinsic existence* (in Tibetan, this is literally "self-emptiness"). We should not, however, understand this self-emptiness or emptiness of self-nature to mean that form is empty *of itself;* this would be tantamount to denying the reality of form, which, as I have been repeatedly emphasizing, these teachings do not do. Form *is* form; the reality of form being form is not being rejected, only the *independent and thus intrinsic existence* of that reality is rejected. Thus, the fact that form is form does not contradict in any way the fact that form is emptiness.

This is a crucial point, and is worth reiteration. Emptiness does not imply non-existence; emptiness implies the emptiness of *intrinsic* existence, which necessarily implies dependent origination. Dependence and interdependence is the nature of all things; things and events come into being only as a result of causes and conditions. Emptiness makes the law of cause and effect possible.

We can express all of this in yet another way as the following chain of reasoning. All things originate dependently. Because all things originate dependently, one can observe cause and effect. Cause and effect are only possible in a world that is dependently originated, and dependent origination is only possible in a world that is devoid of intrinsic existence, which is to say in a world that is empty. Therefore, we can say that emptiness is form, which is another way of saying that form arises from emptiness, and emptiness is the basis that allows the dependent origination of form. Thus the world of form is a *manifestation* of emptiness.

It is important to clarify that we are not speaking of emptiness as some kind of absolute stratum of reality, akin to, say, the ancient Indian concept of *Brahman*, which is conceived to be an underlying absolute reality from which the illusory world of multiplicity emerges. Emptiness is not a core reality, lying somehow at the heart of the universe, from which the diversity of phenomena arise. Emptiness can only be conceived of in relation to individual things and events. For example, when we speak of the emptiness of a form, we are talking about the ultimate reality of *that form*, the fact that it is devoid of intrinsic existence. *That emptiness* is the ultimate nature of *that form*. Emptiness exists only as a quality of a particular phenomenon; emptiness does not exist separately and independently of particular phenomena.

Furthermore, since emptiness can only be understood as ultimate reality in relation to individual phenomena, individual things and events, when an individual phenomenon ceases to exist, the emptiness of that phenomenon will also cease to exist. So, although emptiness is not itself the product of causes and conditions, when a basis for identifying emptiness no longer exists, the emptiness of that thing also ceases to exist.[23]

The line "Emptiness is not other than form, form too is not other than emptiness" indicates the necessity of understanding the Buddha's teaching on the two truths. The first of these two truths is the truth of everyday convention, while the second, ultimate truth, is the truth arrived at through analysis into the ultimate mode of being of things.

Nagarjuna makes reference to this in *Fundamentals of the Middle Way:*

The teachings revealed by the buddhas
are done so in terms of the two truths—
the conventional truth of the world
and the ultimate truth.[24]

We perceive conventional truth, that is, the relative world in all its diversity, through our everyday use of mind and our sense faculties. However, it is only through penetrating analysis that we are able to perceive ultimate truth, the true nature of things and events. To perceive this is to perceive the suchness of phenomena, their ultimate mode of being, which is the ultimate truth about the nature of reality. Although many Indian schools of thought—both Buddhist and non-Buddhist—understand the nature of reality in terms of two truths, the more subtle understanding entails the realization of the two truths not as two separate, independent realities but rather as two aspects of a single reality. It is essential that we clearly grasp this distinction.

TRADITIONS OF INTERPRETATION

One commentarial tradition—perhaps stemming from the Nyingma master Ju Mipham—has a customary way of reading this passage of the *Heart Sutra* presenting the *four approaches to understanding emptiness*. According to this reading, the first statement, "form is emptiness," presents the emptiness of the phenomenal world, thereby countering the extreme of existential absolutism, the mistaken belief that all phenomena have absolute reality. The second statement, "emptiness is form," presents emptiness as arising as dependent origination, thereby countering the extreme of nihilism, the mistaken belief that nothing exists. The third statement, "Emptiness is not other than form," presents the union of appearance and emptiness, or the union of emptiness and dependent origination, countering both extremes, nihilism and existential absolutism, at once. The fourth statement, "form too is not other than emptiness," indicates that appearance and emptiness are not incompatible, abiding instead in a state of total unanimity. Thus, these four aspects are understood as presenting total transcendence of all conceptual elaborations.

The Path and Fruition *(Lamdré)* tradition of the Sakya school of Tibetan Buddhism presents a similar fourfold approach to understanding emptiness: (i) appearance is established as empty; (ii) emptiness is affirmed as dependent origination; (iii) emptiness and appearance are affirmed as a unity; and (iv) this unity is affirmed as transcending all linguistic expression and conceptual thought.

Normally, emptiness is said to be an antidote to the appearance of intrinsic existence, but this fourfold approach indicates that, if one's understanding is sufficiently deep, one will be able to use the truth of emptiness to counter nihilistic views, and use the affirmation of the world of appearance as a way to overcome absolutism. This reverse way of transcending the two extremes is a unique feature of the Prasangika Madhyamaka School.

After setting out this fourfold approach to understanding emptiness, the *Heart Sutra* suggests that, just as one applies this approach to understanding the emptiness of form, one should extend it to the remaining aggregates—feelings, perceptions, mental formations, and consciousness. In the category of the five aggregates are included all composite phenomena.

Likewise, feelings, perceptions, mental formations, and consciousness are all empty.

One way to understand this passage is from the perspective of a meditator realizing emptiness directly. Such a person directly perceives the complete absence of independent reality of all things and events, directly perceiving emptiness alone. In such a state, no multiplicity is experienced: there is no form, no feelings, no sensation, no perception, no mental formations—nor anything else at all.

There is nothing but emptiness because this insight is arrived at only through the process of negating the intrinsic reality of, for instance, form. Form is a conventional reality, a relative phenomenon, and relative phenomena are only known through conventional perception. However, the emptiness of the form is the ultimate truth or ultimate reality of that form. And that ultimate reality is attained only through an ultimate analysis, only through the mind that realizes the ultimate nature of reality. While the mind perceives emptiness directly, it perceives nothing else, and so within such a perspective there is no longer subject and object.

Were form found to exist at the end of one's ultimate analysis, at the end of one's process of negation, then form could be said to be the ultimate nature of itself. This, however, is not the case. The ultimate nature of form is emptiness, and form is the conventional reality upon which that emptiness is established. Therefore one way of reading this statement—that there is no form, no feelings, no sensation, no perception, no mental formations, in emptiness—is from the perspective of a meditator immersed in the direct realization of emptiness.

THE EIGHT ASPECTS OF EMPTINESS

The text of the *Heart Sutra* then presents what are called the *eight aspects of the profound:*

> Therefore, Shariputra, all phenomena are emptiness; they are without defining characteristics; they are not born, they do not cease; they are not defiled, they are not undefiled; they are not deficient, and they are not complete.

"Defining characteristics" in this passage refers to both the universal qualities of phenomena, such as impermanence and emptiness, and the specific characteristics of any given phenomena—such as the characteristics of, say, a particular apple. Both kinds of characteristics exist on the relative level—and indeed we define all things and events by means of such characteristics—but they do not exist in an absolute sense as ultimate natures of things and events.

The text goes on to say that all things " they are not born, they do not cease." It is important to understand that things and events *do* come into being and have origination; arising and ceasing to exist are characteristics of all phenomena—but these characteristics do not exist as ultimate natures of those things. Again, from the perspective of a person immersed in the direct realization of emptiness, characteristics such as origination and cessation are not found; such characteristics do not inhere in things in an ultimate sense.

This insight is reiterated in Nagarjuna's salutation verse at the beginning of *Fundamentals of the Middle Way,* where we read:

He who taught dependent origination—
no cessation and no origination,
no annihilation and no permanence,
no coming and no going,
neither different nor same—
this thorough calming of conceptual elaborations:
To you, who is supreme speaker
among all fully enlightened buddhas, I pay homage.[25]

Here, Nagarjuna pays homage to the Buddha for teaching that a dependently originated thing lacks eight characteristics and is thereby free of intrinsic existence. These eight characteristics *do* exist as qualities of things and events on the conventional level; that is, phenomena do conventionally cease and are conventionally born, and so on, but these characteristics *do not* inhere in them on the ultimate level. On the ultimate level, there is only the *absence* of these characteristics—namely, absence of intrinsic nature, absence of defining characteristics, absence of origination, absence of cessation, absence of defilement, absence of non-defilement, absence of decrease, and absence of increase.

These eight characteristics can be grouped into three categories, each examining emptiness from a different perspective. These three perspectives are called the *three doors of liberation*. If we look at emptiness from the point of view of the thing itself, we see that all phenomena are empty of intrinsic nature and empty of self-defining characteristics. Seeing this is the first door of liberation, the *door of emptiness*. If we look at emptiness from the point of view of its cause, we see that it is unborn, unceasing, not defiled, and not undefiled. This is the second door of liberation, the *door of signlessness*. If we look at emptiness from the point of view of its effects, we see there is no deficiency and no completeness. This is the third door of liberation, the *door of wishlessness*.

These three doors are in actuality three ways of understanding the same thing: emptiness. The scriptures state that the wisdom that realizes emptiness is the one true door, the only way we can become completely free from the grasp of ignorance and the suffering it causes.

CHAPTER 11

Attaining the Result

The Emptiness of All Phenomena

Let us return to the text of the *Heart Sutra:*

> Therefore, Shariputra, in emptiness there is no form, no
> feelings, no perceptions, no mental formations, and no con-
> sciousness. There is no eye, no ear, no nose, no tongue, no
> body, and no mind. There is no form, no sound, no smell,
> no taste, no texture, and no mental objects. There is no eye-
> element and so on up to no mind-element including up to
> no element of mental consciousness.

The first sentence here reaffirms the emptiness of the five
aggregates, while the next sentence extends this emptiness to the six
faculties—the five sensory faculties and the mental faculty. The subsequent sentence extends emptiness further, to external objects—the
sensory bases of form, sound, smell, taste, texture, and mental
objects. The final sentence extends this further still—to the emptiness of the eighteen elements, culminating with there being "no element of mental consciousness."[26] All things and events, including
noncomposite phenomena such as space, are included within these

categories; thus all phenomena are devoid of intrinsic existence. The
text then reads:

> There is no ignorance, there is no extinction of ignorance
> and so on up to no aging and death and no extinction of
> aging and death.

This is a summary negation of the twelve links of dependent
origination in accordance with their sequence of evolution within
the chain of an unenlightened existence. Although just two are mentioned specifically, the implication "and so on" is to be read as
negating all twelve of the links—ignorance, volitional action, consciousness, name and form, sense sources, contact, feelings, attachment, craving, becoming, birth, and aging and death. The negation
of these twelve links describes the process of attaining nirvana.
Although both the process for taking birth in the cycle of existence
and the process of gaining freedom from it do exist on the conventional level, they do not exist on an ultimate level; thus they are
negated here. The text goes on to read:

> Likewise, there is no suffering, origin, cessation, or path; there
> is no wisdom, no attainment, and even no non-attainment.

This begins with a negation, again from the perspective of thoroughly realized emptiness, of the first turning of the Dharma
wheel—the four noble truths: the truth of suffering, its origin, its
cessation, and the path to its cessation. Thus, meditative practice is
negated. Next, the fruition of this practice is negated—"there is no
wisdom, no attainment"—by affirming the emptiness of the

subjective experience. Finally even this negation is itself negated—
"no non-attainment." Even the resultant state of clarity that arises
from clear penetration into the perfection of wisdom is itself empty
of intrinsic existence. All the qualities of the mind of one who has
reached nirvana or attained the supernatural powers of a buddha—
these are empty and are negated here.

Nirvana

The text then reads:

> Therefore, Shariputra, since bodhisattvas have no attainments,
> they rely on this perfection of wisdom and abide in it. Hav-
> ing no obscuration in their minds, they have no fear, and by
> going utterly beyond error, they will reach the end of nirvana.

In the context of the *Heart Sutra*, we understand nirvana to be the
ultimate nature of one's mind at a stage when the mind has become
totally cleansed of all mental afflictions. As we have seen earlier, it
is because the mind is innately pure, which is to say it has buddha
nature, that simply removing the obscurations to clarity reveals
enlightenment; thus, the emptiness of the mind is said to be the
basis of nirvana, its *natural nirvana*. When an individual goes through
a process of purifying the mind by applying the antidotes to the
mental afflictions, over time, the mind becomes totally free of all
these obscurations. The emptiness of this undefiled mind is the *true
nirvana* or liberation. Thus, one can attain liberation—true nirvana—
only through actualizing the ultimate nature of the mind in its perfect and unafflicted state.

As Nagarjuna explains in *Fundamentals of the Middle Way*, emptiness is therefore both the means of eliminating the mental afflictions and the resultant state that one arrives at after having done so. Nagarjuna writes:

Through cessation of karma and afflictions one is freed.
Karma, afflictions, and conceptualization
all arise from elaboration; and it is by means of emptiness
that elaboration is brought to an end.[27]

Since all the aspects of one's path to enlightenment—one's innate capacity to attain enlightenment through the path, the path itself, and the results of the path to enlightenment—are devoid of intrinsic existence, they all possess natural nirvana. Through cultivating insight into this natural nirvana, one will be able to dispel and overcome the sufferings resulting from the erroneous understanding of things and events, which is to say, resulting from fundamental ignorance. Not only can the sufferings be removed, but even the propensity for self-grasping ignorance and the imprints left by past ignorant actions can be removed. Thus, one can completely eliminate ignorance in the present, the imprints of it from the past, and the propensity toward ignorance in the future. Transcending all ignorance, the sutra goes on to tell us, one naturally becomes free of fear, and one abides in the final and non-abiding nirvana of a buddha.

All the buddhas too who abide in the three times attained the full awakening of unexcelled, perfect enlightenment by relying on this profound perfection of wisdom.

Here, in the phrase "all the buddhas who abide in the three times," the term *buddha* actually refers to bodhisattvas of the highest level of spiritual attainment just prior to the attainment of buddhahood; this level is called the *buddha level*. A bodhisattva on this level, through remaining single-pointedly absorbed in the meditative absorption called *adamantine meditative absorption,* will possess similitude of all the enlightened attributes of a buddha. By remaining in this absorption, such a bodhisattva will, in dependence upon the perfection of wisdom, attain the final awakening of the Buddha.

THE MANTRA OF THE PERFECTION OF WISDOM

Up to this point, the *Heart Sutra* is said to be an explanation of emptiness for trainees who are of unexceptional aptitude. The text then makes a concise presentation, in the form of a mantra, of emptiness, which is aimed at people of the highest aptitude. The text reads:

> Therefore, one should know that the mantra of the perfection of wisdom—the mantra of great knowledge, the unexcelled mantra, the mantra equal to the unequalled, the mantra that quells all suffering—is true because it is not deceptive.

The perfection of wisdom itself, *prajnaparamita*, is here referred to as a "mantra." The etymological meaning of *mantra* is "to protect the mind." Thus, through attaining the perfection of wisdom, one's mind will be completely protected against erroneous beliefs, against the mental afflictions that arise from such beliefs, and against the suffering produced by the mental afflictions.

The perfection of wisdom is called the "mantra of great knowledge" because thoroughly understanding its meaning eliminates the three poisons of craving, hatred, and delusion. It is called the "unexcelled mantra" because there is no greater method than the perfection of wisdom for saving one from the extremes of cyclic existence and the isolated peace of individual nirvana. It is called the mantra "equal to the unequalled" because the Buddha's enlightened state is unequalled, and, through the deepest realization of this mantra, one attains a state equal to that state. Finally, the perfection of wisdom is known as the "mantra that quells all suffering" because it quells manifest sufferings and also removes all propensities for future suffering.

The perfection of wisdom is the ultimate truth, thus the statement "it is true." In the realm of the ultimate truth, there is no disparity, as there is in conventional reality, between appearance and reality, and thus this manifest ultimate truth is "not deceptive." This nondeceptiveness also suggests that, through actualization of this mantra, the perfection of wisdom can enable one to attain total freedom from suffering and its causes. From this perspective too, we can say that it is the truth.

The mantra of the perfection of wisdom is proclaimed: *tadyatha gaté gaté paragaté parasamgaté bodhi svaha!* Shariputra, the bodhisattvas, the great beings, should train in the perfection of wisdom in this way.

In Sanskrit, *tadyatha* literally means "it is thus" and prepares the way for what follows; *gaté gaté* means "go, go"; *paragaté* means "go beyond"; *parasamgaté* means "go totally beyond"; and *bodhi svaha* can be read as "be rooted in the ground of enlightenment." Thus, the entire mantra itself can be translated as "Go, go, go beyond, go totally beyond, be rooted in the ground of enlightenment." We can interpret this mantra metaphorically to read "Go to the other shore," which is to say, abandon this shore of samsara, unenlightened existence, which has been our home since beginningless time, and cross to the other shore of final nirvana and complete liberation.

THE IMPLICIT MEANING OF THE HEART SUTRA

The mantra contains the implicit, or hidden, meaning of the *Heart Sutra*, revealing how the understanding of emptiness is related to the five stages of the path to buddhahood. In this mantra, we can read the first "go" as an exhortation to enter the path of accumulating merit, and the second as an exhortation to the path of preparing the mind to deeply perceive emptiness. "Go beyond" refers to the path of seeing reality, the direct and unmediated realization of emptiness. A practitioner who sees in this way has become an *arya*, or noble being. "Go totally beyond" indicates the path of meditation (*gom* in Tibetan, literally "habituation"), wherein one becomes deeply familiar with emptiness through constant practice. The final part of this mantra, "bodhi svaha," is an exhortation to establish oneself firmly in the ground of enlightenment, which is to say, enter final nirvana.

We can relate these five stages on the path to buddhahood—accumulation, preparation, seeing, meditation, and no more learning—to the different parts of the main body of the *Heart Sutra*. The fourfold presentation of emptiness at the beginning of the sutra—"form is emptiness, emptiness is form. Emptiness is not other than form, form is also not other than emptiness"—presents the way to practice emptiness at the first two stages—accumulation and preparation. The emptiness of the eight aspects of phenomena—"all phenomena are emptiness; they are without defining characteristics," and so on—presents the mode of generating insight into emptiness at the stage of seeing. The phrase "There is no ignorance, there is no extinction of ignorance," and so on, explains the method of practicing emptiness at the level of the stage of meditation. The next section, "Therefore, Shariputra, since bodhisattvas have no attainments, they rely on this perfection of wisdom and abide in it," explains the practice of emptiness on the last bodhisattva level, where the bodhisattva abides in adamantine meditative absorption.

The actual transition from one stage to the next takes place when the practitioner is immersed in meditative equipoise. At the initial stage, that is when the practitioner is on the path of accumulation, one's understanding of emptiness is derived more from intellectual understanding of emptiness and the nature of phenomena. Bodhisattva practitioners with keen intellects may attain significant understanding of emptiness prior to generating the altruistic attitude of bodhichitta; those less inclined toward intellection may develop the aspiration to liberate all beings first. In either case, a profound understanding of emptiness will powerfully impact other areas of practice, reinforcing and complementing them. A deep understanding of emptiness can lead to powerful renunciation, which is the aspiration to free oneself from the suffering of cyclic existence, and it can serve also as the basis for cultivating strong compassion toward all beings.

In the stage of accumulation, one's realization of emptiness is derived primarily from learning, reflection, and intellectual understanding; and through meditation on what one has learned, one's understanding becomes deeper and deeper, until one ultimately gains a total clarity of insight. At this point, one enters the stage of preparation. Here, the individual's insight into emptiness, while not yet direct, is no longer intellectual or conceptual but rather experiential.

During the stage of preparation, one's understanding of emptiness becomes progressively deeper, subtler, and clearer. The use of concepts in meditation gradually recedes. When all dualistic perceptions of subject and object, of conventional reality, and of intrinsic existence are removed, one enters the path of seeing. At this point, there is no separation of subject and object; it is as if the subjective experience and its object have become fused, like water poured into water, and one's meditation on emptiness becomes unmediated and direct.

As one's direct experience of emptiness deepens, one systematically counters the various mental afflictions during the stage of meditation, or familiarization. During this stage, one progresses through what are known as the *seven impure bodhisattva levels*. They are called impure because the mental afflictions are not fully eradicated until the eighth level. On the eighth, ninth, and tenth levels, one counters even the propensities and imprints left by the afflictions. Finally, when one removes the obscuration preventing the simultaneous perception of both ultimate and conventional truth within a single cognitive event, the omniscient mind of a buddha dawns.

ALL REJOICE

The recitation of the perfection of wisdom mantra concludes Avalokiteshvara's answer to Shariputra's question in the opening section of the *Heart Sutra*. Thus far, we have discussed the inspired scripture, and from this point on, we will discuss the expression of rejoicing, which belongs to the category of spoken scriptures, those teachings spoken by the Buddha himself.

> Thereupon, the Blessed One arose from that meditative absorption and commended the holy Avalokiteshvara, the bodhisattva, the great being, saying this is excellent. "Excellent! Excellent! O noble child, it is just so; it should be just so. One must practice the profound perfection of wisdom just as you have revealed. For then even the tathagatas will rejoice."

Up to this point, the Buddha has been deeply immersed in meditative absorption on the appearance of the profound. Without any volition on his part, the Buddha inspires Avalokiteshvara and Shariputra to engage in the foregoing dialogue. When their dialogue is concluded, the Buddha commends and affirms Avalokiteshvara's expression. This affirmation indicates that Buddha's meditative absorption is in fact a fusion of both deep meditative equipoise upon emptiness—ultimate truth—and full cognizance of the world of phenomena continually unfolding—conventional truth. This simultaneous awareness is a unique quality of the mind of a buddha.

The *Heart of Wisdom Sutra* concludes as follows:

> As the Blessed One uttered these words, the venerable Shariputra, the holy Avalokiteshvara, the bodhisattva, the great being, along with the entire assembly, including the worlds of gods, humans, asuras, and gandharvas, all rejoiced and hailed what the Blessed One had said.

When we read and endeavor to thoroughly grasp the depth of meaning of a scripture such as this one, we can begin to appreciate the deep sentiments expressed in homages to the Buddha. Out of the most profound depths of his realization, Tsongkhapa, the great fourteenth-century meditator and scholar, wrote the following lines, expressing heartfelt admiration and boundless gratitude for the Buddha's teaching on the profound truth of emptiness:

> And yet, as I contemplate your words,
> the thought arises in me:
> "Ah, this teacher, enveloped in a halo of light
> and brilliant with the glorious major and minor marks,
> has taught thus in his perfect *brahma* melody."
> O Buddha, as your image reflects in my mind,
> it brings solace to my weary heart,
> like the cool moon rays to one tormented by heat.[28]

Part III

The Way of the Bodhisattva

CHAPTER 12

Generating Bodhichitta

A GRADUAL APPROACH

WE NEED a gradual approach to our spiritual training in order to make progress in our spiritual and mental development toward a highly disciplined and deeply realized state of mind. We see this gradual process of development everywhere, both in the physical world and also in the inner realm of the mind. In fact, gradual development appears to be a natural law, a corollary, as it were, to the law of cause and effect. This gradual mental transformation and spiritual development must take place on the basis of what Buddhists call the union of method (*upaya*) and wisdom (*prajna*). The *Heart Sutra* is a wonderful presentation of wisdom, and we've examined it in depth. Now, let's pay some attention to method, specifically with regard to developing compassion.

In order for the wisdom of emptiness to serve as a completely effective antidote to both the mental afflictions and the subtle obscurations to knowledge, one must have the complementary factor of *bodhichitta*, the altruistic intention to attain buddhahood for the benefit of all beings. Bodhichitta, the method aspect of the path, is a critical factor necessary to attain the omniscient mind of full enlightenment—the mind of a fully awakened buddha. Furthermore, it can be said that bodhichitta is the defining characteristic of a bodhisattva, or what the *Heart Sutra* calls "a noble son or noble daughter."

One may have a deep, valid understanding of emptiness, and one may even have attained freedom from cyclic existence; however, as long as one lacks bodhichitta, one is not a bodhisattva. In order to generate this bodhichitta, it is not adequate to merely wish compassionately that other sentient beings be happy and free of suffering. It is necessary to have a deep sense of commitment that *I myself* will take up the responsibility to free all other beings from suffering. In order to generate such powerful compassion, one first needs to develop a sense of intimacy and empathy with other sentient beings; without true intimacy, genuine bodhichitta cannot arise. We will examine what this intimacy entails below.

The great Indian masters of Nalanda Monastery set out two principal methods for generating *bodhichitta:* the seven-point cause-and-effect method and the method of equalizing and exchanging self and others.

THE SEVEN-POINT CAUSE-AND-EFFECT METHOD

In the seven-point cause-and-effect method, you visualize every being as your own beloved mother or as another person for whom you have the utmost affection—someone who for you embodies great kindness. To practice this aspect of the method, call up the feelings of affection that arise with regard to one's mother or another maternally kind and loving person and then extend those feelings to every other being, perceiving that each being has been equally kind and loving to you. When we truly realize our interconnectedness over the scope of beginningless lifetimes, we realize that every other being has been our parent and has treated us with this same loving and nurturing kindness.

We can observe what this type of kindness entails by looking to the animal kingdom. If we carefully observe birds, for instance, carefully, we see that until offspring are capable of taking care of themselves, the mother takes them under her wing and nurses them. Irrespective of whether she really has what we humans call compassion, this act alone is doubtlessly immense kindness from the mother. The offspring are totally dependent upon the mother; they behave as if she is their sole protector, their sole refuge, and their sole provider. Furthermore, the mother is so dedicated to the well-being of her offspring that she would be willing, if necessary, to sacrifice her own life in order to protect them. It is this spirit that we need to cultivate in regard to all beings.

Contemplation of beginningless lifetimes allows us to recognize that all sentient beings have acted in this very manner toward us, in some capacity and to some degree. Appreciating this, we develop a strong sense of empathy and gratitude toward other sentient beings, which, in turn, enables us to feel a greater sense of genuine closeness with them. Feeling this closeness, we are able to perceive their kindness to us, regardless of how they may behave toward us at present. This is what is meant by genuine intimacy with all beings.

But, like all other things, this intimacy comes gradually. The first stage is the cultivation of a sense of equanimity toward all beings. In our normal, everyday state of mind, our emotions and attitudes toward others fluctuate wildly—we feel close to some people and distant from others; our feelings even for a single person may move from one extreme to the other as some small circumstance changes.

But, if we have not purged our mind of the afflictions, our everyday sense of closeness is inevitably grounded in delusion, in attachment. Closeness grounded in attachment can actually obstruct our generation of true compassion. Thus, we begin by cultivating equanimity. Then, having cultivated equanimity, we cultivate a sense of closeness to others grounded in sound reasoning rather than attachment.

Over time, we generate such a sense of intimacy that we cannot stand that other beings are suffering. Eventually, our great compassion, our heartfelt wish to see others free from suffering, becomes so powerful that we make the commitment that we ourselves will bring about their release from suffering. And likewise we generate lovingkindness—the wish that others enjoy happiness—and again make the commitment that we ourselves will bring this about. Ultimately, when we have generated such powerful compassion and lovingkindness along with a sense of personal commitment, we give rise to the "extraordinary altruistic attitude" that seeks to release all beings from suffering by oneself alone. Once we have cultivated this extraordinary attitude, we can analyze whether we actually possess the capacity to bring about others' ultimate well-being. The great Indian logician Dharmakirti says in his *Exposition of Valid Cognition (Pramanavarttika)*:

> If the factors pertaining to the means remain obscure,
> It is difficult to explain them to others.[29]

From a Buddhist point of view, the most effective way to ensure the ultimate welfare of all other sentient beings is to lead them to buddhahood. However, in order to lead them to that goal, we must have both the knowledge and actual realization of it ourselves.

Reflecting in this way, we come to recognize that in order to secure the ultimate welfare of all sentient beings, we ourselves must attain enlightenment. This very thought, the culmination of the seven-point practice, is bodhichitta. It is endowed with both the aspiration to bring about others' welfare and the aspiration to attain buddhahood for that purpose.

EQUALIZING AND EXCHANGING ONESELF AND OTHERS

Another method, equalizing and exchanging oneself and others, involves cultivating a deep recognition of the fundamental sameness of oneself and others. In fact, as far as the natural wish to seek happiness and to overcome suffering is concerned, oneself and others are absolutely identical. We should cultivate the thought "Just as I myself have the right to fulfil the basic aspiration to be happy and overcome suffering, so too do others; just as I have the potential to fulfil this aspiration, so too do others." The difference between oneself and all others lies only in number: one case refers to but a single individual, and the other to countless beings. We then ask, therefore, whose need is greater?

Often, when we think about our own interests versus the interests of others, we have a notion that the two are unrelated. This is not the case. Since everyone is part of a community, a complex social fabric, any negative event in an individual's life impacts the entire community. Likewise, anything that affects a community affects each member individually as well.

Furthermore, consider the following line of reasoning: If, by perpetually harboring self-cherishing thoughts we could fulfill our self-centered aspirations to achieve our own happiness, then, because we have done this ceaselessly since our birth and over countless lifetimes, we surely would have succeeded by now. But, of course, we have not succeeded. We must therefore conclude that using our minds in our accustomed self-centered ways will never bring us ultimate happiness or liberate even our own cherished self from suffering.

In contrast, Shantideva states in the *Guide to the Bodhisattva's Way of Life* that if, at some point in the past, we had reversed our way of being, discarding our self-cherishing and adopting instead the thought of cherishing others' well-being, pursuing the path with this changed perspective, we would have attained the fully enlightened state by now. He writes:

> If you had in some remote past
> accomplished acts such as this,
> other than the bliss of the Buddha's perfection,
> this situation of today would not be.[30]

SELF-CHERISHING VERSUS CHERISHING OTHERS

In the *Precious Garland* (*Ratnavali*), Nagarjuna states that for those wishing to attain the omniscient state of a buddha, it is essential to uphold three foundational principles—great compassion, which is the root; bodhichitta, which arises from great compassion; and the wisdom realizing emptiness, which is the key factor that complements the other two.

All great beings, like Buddha Shakyamuni, have recognized the shortcomings of self-cherishing and have recognized the benefits of cultivating the thought of cherishing the well-being of others. In contrast, we continue to live in a cycle of suffering that rolls on unceasingly like waves on the ocean—even before one wave ends, another arises. Although we complain about suffering, we are caught in this cycle because we have entrusted our entire well-being to this extremely self-centered attitude and because we have allied ourselves with the traitorous attitude of grasping at self-existence.

At the root of all suffering lie two powerful forces: self-grasping—the deluded grasping at an intrinsically real self—and the self-centered thought that cherishes only one's own welfare. These two attitudes reside deep within the innermost recesses of our hearts and there join forces and hold unchallenged dominion over our lives. Unless we actively seek to perfect our understanding of emptiness and our compassion for others, this dominion will remain as hard and unchanging as a diamond.

It is important that we not misunderstand this altruistic ideal of cherishing other sentient beings. We should not understand it to imply that we should totally sacrifice or give up our own interests. In fact, if we look at the practice of bodhichitta, we see that cultivation of this altruistic aspiration is accompanied by the aspiration to attain full enlightenment, which ultimately represents the highest fulfilment of one's own interests. Full enlightenment has two aspects, embodied by the union of the "form body" (*rupakaya*) and the "body of reality," or the "truth body" (*dharmakaya*). The body of reality represents the fulfillment of one's own self-interest, while the form body represents the fulfillment of the welfare of other sentient beings. Similarly, the great Tibetan Buddhist master Tsongkhapa points out that when one helps other sentient beings, one's own wishes are fulfilled as a by-product. In fact, pursuing the greatest interests of others is the wisest way to pursue one's own interests.

The Practice of Giving and Taking

On the basis of having developed profound empathy toward others, one can then engage in the practice of *tong len*, which is Tibetan for "giving and taking." In this practice, one imagines taking upon oneself all of the suffering and potential suffering of others, while giving them all of one's happiness and positive potential. The practice of taking primarily enhances compassion, while the practice of giving primarily enhances lovingkindness. It is open to question how effective such a practice is in directly benefiting the object of one's meditation, although that may be possible where a strong karmic connection between individuals exists. What *is* certain, however, is that the practice of tong len can have tremendous impact on increasing one's own courage and determination to fulfill the bodhisattva aspiration. Further, tong len decreases the force of the self-cherishing attitude, while enhancing the force of the thought that cherishes the well-being of others. When trained through the approach of exchanging and equalizing self and others, this practice too can give birth to the extraordinary altruistic attitude, and ultimately to bodhichitta itself.

Generating Bodhichitta

Again let me emphasize that the development of bodhichitta is gradual. It begins at the level of intellectual understanding derived primarily from hearing or studying the teachings. As we continue to reflect upon bodhichitta on the intellectual level, at a certain point, we may begin to feel a deeper sense of conviction in the noble ideals of bodhichitta. We will have then attained what might be called a reflective level of experience. As we go more deeply into this contemplation and understanding, we will reach a point where we genuinely and accurately comprehend at least the ideal, or sentiment, of bodhichitta. Comprehending this, we become able to fully practice the thought processes of cultivating bodhichitta and feel a powerful inner impact; at that point we will have attained the bodhichitta that arises through effort—but this simulated bodhichitta is not yet true bodhichitta. Only through much additional practice can we reach the point where bodhichitta arises spontaneously. At this point, we no longer need to go through a deliberate thought process in order for bodhichitta to arise; a simple triggering thought or some external stimulus can give rise to this powerful emotion. This genuine bodhichitta is the bodhichitta of the bodhisattva, and by attaining it one becomes a bodhisattva oneself.

Afterword

WHEN THIS SERIES of lectures was originally delivered, I had the wonderful opportunity to listen to chanting from members of several different Buddhist traditions at the beginning of each session. Historically, the Theravada, the main tradition of Sri Lanka and Southeast Asia, is senior among the followers of our most compassionate and skillful teacher, Buddha Shakyamuni, and they have preserved the Buddha's teachings in the Pali language. I also heard chanting from members of the Chinese Buddhist tradition, the primary source of which is the Sanskrit tradition and, to some extent, the Pali as well. This was then followed by chanting from the members of the Vietnamese monastic tradition. Most of these different traditions of Buddhism predate Tibetan Buddhism. So, appropriately, last, I had the chance to listen to Tibetan chanting.

I was deeply moved and also very grateful to be part of this precious occasion, where representatives of the various Buddhist traditions—all students of the same teacher, Buddha Shakyamuni—performed chants from a single platform. It is important to note that in China, Buddhism has historically been one of the dominant religions of the land. The chanting of Buddhist scripture in Chinese highlighted the spiritual aspirations of millions of human beings in that country who continue to have faith in the teachings of the Buddha. In the past few decades, there has been great damage to the Buddhadharma in that great country. However, the rich Chinese cultural traditions, including the Buddhist faith, are still very much alive today.

As time passes, although many newer ideologies and systems fail, the values of Buddhism, and of all major world religions, are still very much alive in human society, and in the lives and hearts of individual human beings. I think this is a sign of hope for the human family, for within the values of our religions lie the keys to a more just and peaceful world for generations to follow. I offer my prayers that these positive aspects of the world's religions may increase in the minds of their practitioners, and that religion may no longer be used as a basis for conflict and strife, but rather for greater understanding and cooperation among the earth's inhabitants, and that through individual effort, we may each secure the welfare of all.

Appendix

Thorough Elucidation
of the Meaning of the Words:
An Exposition of the "Heart of Wisdom"[31]

Jamyang Gawai Lodrö (1429–1503)

Respectfully, I pay homage to the lotus feet of the most holy Manjushri.

> Having bowed to the conqueror who taught that there are not two but only one path trodden by all the buddhas and their children, I shall elucidate here briefly the words of the *Heart [of Wisdom]*, which is the most cherished treasury of all his teachings.

Here, the exposition of the *Heart of Wisdom* has four sections:

1. The meaning of its title
2. Homage by the translator
3. Subject matter of the main text
4. Conclusion

The first refers to "In Indian language…," etc, the understanding of which is easy.

The second [the homage by the translator] refers to "Homage to the Bhagavati, the perfection of wisdom." This has been inserted by the translator.

Subject Matter of the Main Text

The third [the subject matter of the main text] consists of two sections:

I. Prologue indicating the origination of the sutra
II. Subject matter of the actual sutra thus evolved

Prologue

The first is twofold:

A. Common prologue
B. Uncommon prologue

The first [the common prologue] refers to the coming together of the *four perfect factors.* "Thus have I once heard" indicates the perfect factor of time; "The Blessed One" indicates the perfect factor of teacher; "In Rajaghriha at Vulture Peak" indicates the perfect factor of place; and "along with a great community of monks…bodhisattvas" indicates the perfect factor of retinues. These are easy to understand.

The second [the uncommon prologue] refers to [the following two passages:] "at that time, the Blessed One entered the meditative absorption on the varieties of phenomena called the appearance of the profound" and "At that time as well, the noble Avalokiteshvara, the bodhisattva, the great being, clearly beheld the practice of the profound perfection of wisdom and saw that even the five aggregates are empty of intrinsic existence." The teacher abided in meditative absorption and through his blessing inspired the following queries and responses.

SUBJECT MATTER OF THE ACTUAL SUTRA

The subject matter of the actual sutra, which is the perfect teaching, has four parts:

A. Shariputra's question on the mode of practicing the perfection of wisdom

B. Avalokiteshvara's responses

C. The teacher's affirmation of this

D. The assembly members' delight and their pledge to uphold[32]

The first [Shariputra's question] is [presented in the following]: "Thereupon, through the Buddha's inspiration, the venerable Shariputra spoke to the noble Avalokiteshvara, the bodhisattva, the great being, and said, 'How should any noble son or noble daughter who wishes to engage in the practice of the profound perfection of wisdom train?'" The question is thus raised. This is a question pertaining to the mode of training in the [bodhisattva] practices in the aftermath of generating the mind [of awakening] for those who possess the inclination toward the great vehicle.

The second—how the replies were given—has three parts:

1. Individual presentation of the mode of training in the path to those of inferior faculties
2. Presentation through mere words of *mantra* to those of superior faculties
3. Exhortation to train by means of summarizing the subject matter

The first consists of [the following]:

a. Presentation of the mode of training in the perfection of wisdom on the path of accumulation and the path of preparation
b. Presentation of the mode of training on the path of seeing
c. Presentation of the mode of training on the path of meditation
d. Presentation of the mode of training on the path of no more learning

TRAINING ON THE PATHS OF ACCUMULATION AND PREPARATION

The first is composed of:

(1) Transition
(2) Mode of training in the [ultimate] nature of the aggregate of form
(3) Extending the same analysis to the remaining aggregates

The first [the transition] is presented in the following: "When this had been said, the holy Avalokiteshvara, the bodhisattva, the great being, spoke to the venerable Shariputra and said, 'Shariputra, any noble son or noble daughter who so wishes to engage in the practice of the profound perfection of wisdom should clearly see this way.'" Thus by stating that this is how one should see on the path of accumulation and the path of preparation, a transition [between the Shariputra's question and Avalokiteshvara's response] is provided.

The second [the mode of training in the ultimate nature of the aggregate of form] is [first] presented in a concise form in the following: "They should see perfectly that even the five aggregates are empty of intrinsic existence."[33]

"In what manner are [phenomena] empty of intrinsic existence?" [Answer] "Form is devoid of intrinsic existence; while being empty of intrinsic nature, it still appears as form. Emptiness is not other than the aggregate of form; form too is not of separate nature from emptiness."[34] Thus by presenting the two truths to be of one reality but with two aspects, they are revealed to be free of the extremes of absolutism and nihilism.

The third [extending the same analysis to the remaining aggregates] is presented in the passage "Likewise, feelings...consciousness are all empty." With these the remaining aggregates are taught to be viewed in the same manner. This is known as the *fourfold emptiness* and [is also] referred to as the *profound endowed with four aspects*. The point being stressed here is that one views [emptiness] on the path of accumulation primarily through hearing and reflection, and on the path of preparation principally through understanding derived from meditation.

Training on the Path of Seeing

The second [training on the path of seeing] is presented in the passage "Therefore, Shariputra, all phenomena are emptiness; they are without defining characteristics...they are not complete." This is known as the *profound endowed with eight aspects*. By refuting eight aspects of the object of negation, this [passage] presents the mode of entering the three doors of thorough liberation on the path of seeing. This is stated in the oral instructions of the great master [Atisha], which has been put into writing by Ngok Lekshe in his concise presentation.[35]

"All phenomena are emptiness" presents the *emptiness door of thorough liberation*, while the five "They are without defining characteristics; they are not born, they do not cease; they are not defiled, they are not undefiled" present the *signlessness door of thorough liberation*. This is because it presents the absence of the five signs—the signifying characteristics of cause, the absence of origination and cessation of the effects, which are the signified, the absence of the thoroughly afflicted class of phenomena, which is the defiled, and the absence of the enlightened class of phenomena, which are free of defilements. [The phrase] "They are not deficient" presents the *wishlessness [door of thorough liberation]* of the results.

Training on the Path of Meditation

The third—training on the path of meditation—has two parts:

(1) Mode of training on the path of meditation in general
(2) Mode of training in the causal diamond-like [absorption]

The first [the mode of training on the path of meditation in general] is presented in the passage "Therefore, Shariputra, in emptiness, there is no form...and even no non-attainment." Vimalamitra adds a preceding adverbial phrase, thus reading this as "Therefore, at that point, in emptiness, there is no form." He reads this as stating that the path of meditation, which is the continuum of the habituation, arises as a fruit of actualizing the three doors of thorough liberation on the path of seeing by means of refuting the eight objects of negation. Citing thus, the question is raised: "What kinds of perception arise on the path of meditation whilst one is immersed in meditative equipoise insofar as the perspectives of that meditative equipoise are concerned?" It is revealed that "from form to attainments and non-attainments" [phenomena] do not appear as any [of these]. Vimala then cites [the passage] "To see all phenomena is to see emptiness."[36]

The non-observance of the five aggregates is presented in the passage "There is no form, no feelings..." up to "...no consciousness." The non-observance of the twelve sources is presented in the passage "There is no eye...no mental objects." The non-observance of the eighteen elements is presented in the passage "There is no eye-element...up to no element of mental consciousness." There is an observation that in the [original] Indian text there exists a concise presentation up to the [class of] faculties and consciousness, however the translator has abbreviated these [here]. I find this view acceptable.

Then the passage "There is no ignorance...and no extinction of aging and death" presents the absence of the thoroughly afflicted class of phenomena and even the dependent origination of the enlightened class of phenomena insofar as the perspective of the meditative equipoise is concerned. The passage "suffering..." presents the absence of the [four noble] truths, which are the objects of the path. The passage "There is no wisdom..." presents that even the path itself does not exist insofar as this perspective is concerned.[37]

Vimala states that in some versions [of the *Heart Sutra*] there exists the passage "There is no ignorance" as well. If this is so, this should be read as stating that there does not exist even the opposite of wisdom, which is ignorance. A later master, the great Chöje Rongpa, appears to follow a tradition that suggests that there exists in the Indian text the sentence "There is no insight" before [the reference to] wisdom.[38]

The phrase "There is no attainment" indicates the absence of the attainment of such fruits as the [ten] powers and the [four types of] fearlessness. This should be extended also to read "There is no non-attainment as well." Vimala reads this as stating "having negated conceptions of attainment, in order to negate the conceptions pertaining to non-attainment..." The great Chöje Rongpa, however, adds the qualification "On the ultimate level, there is no attainment; yet on the conventional, there is not even non-attainment." He then asserts that this dual formulation should be extended to all [classes of phenomena mentioned] up to this point.

This seems to be an interpretation of the intention of the following statement of Vimala: "One should understand that this [passage] reveals the profound meaning, which is free of the extremes of reification and denigration, by means of going beyond wisdom, ignorance, attainment, and non-attainment." However, since the context here is a discussion of how the perception of form does not arise within the perspective of the meditative equipoise when

probing the nature of reality, [this reflects] Chöje's failure of understanding.

Thus the statement that there is nothing whatsoever—the five
aggregates, the twelve sources, the eighteen elements, the twelve links
of dependent origination, the four noble truths, the nature of the
perceiving paths, the attainment of results, or their non-attainment—
within the perspective of the meditative equipoise, and the statement
that they are devoid of intrinsic existence, share the same meaning.
This is because if form exists within the perspective of the very
awareness that perceives its ultimate mode of being, form then
becomes substantially real. So, in brief, these passages instruct that
on the path of meditation one should abide in equipoise on the single taste of the suchness, which is the total pacification of all dualistic elaborations, such as the conceptualization of form and so on.

The second [the mode of training in the causal diamond-like
meditative absorption] is presented in the following: "Therefore,
Shariputra, since bodhisattvas have no attainments, they rely on this
perfection of wisdom and abide in it."

This is presented in the passage "Having no obscuration in their
minds, they have no fear, and going utterly beyond error, they will
reach the end of nirvana."

Training on the Path of No More Learning

Vimala states that by gradually eliminating the subtle and coarse
obscurations corresponding to the ten [bodhisattva] levels as enu-
merated in the *Sutra Unraveling the Thought of the Buddha*, one becomes
free of the fears born of the four distortions. One thus reaches
beyond them and attains the non-abiding nirvana.[39] The great Chöje

Rongpa, however, reads this as stating "As there is no obscuration of self-grasping in one's mind, there is no fear of emptiness," thus seeming to introduce additional words at will.

If one were to summarize the above, this [section of the text] presents [the following:] On the path of accumulation and the path of preparation, one engages in the practice of emptiness through hearing and reflection and through meditation respectively; while on the path of seeing one actualizes the three doors of thorough liberation by means of refuting the eight objects of negation. On the path of meditation one pacifies all elaborations, such as the conceptualization of form and so on, and travels up to the tenth [bodhisattva] level. One thus eliminates all the defilements corresponding to the ten levels and attains the states of the "three great [objectives]."[40] In this way, it presents the mode of training on the five paths for the trainees of inferior faculties.

Then the passage "All the buddhas too who abide in the three times..." presents the need to train in this very path of all the buddhas. This is easy to understand.

Presentation through Mere Words of Mantra to Those of Superior Faculties

The second [the presentation through mere words of mantra to those of superior faculties] is presented in the passage "Therefore one should know that the mantra of the perfection of wisdom...*svaha*."

Given that the perfection of wisdom contains the meaning of *mantra* (lit. "mind protection"), it is referred to here as a "mantra." Its greatness is as follows: [the mantra] of "great knowledge, the unexcelled mantra, the mantra equal to the unequalled, the mantra that thoroughly quells all suffering," and as it trains one in the [achievement of] one's aspirations, "it must be recognized as the truth." What is this mantra? *"Tadyatha,"* which, like the *om*, brings forth the subsequent words [of the mantra]. *"Gaté gaté"* means "go, go." The first *gaté* indicates [to go on] the path of accumulation and the second to "Go on the path of preparation." *"Paragaté"* means "Go on the path of seeing." *"Parasamgaté"* means "Go perfectly on the other shore, the path of meditation." *"Bodhi svaha"* means "Go perfectly to the great enlightenment and be firmly established."

It is thought that as far as those trainees of higher faculties are concerned, they can understand the mode of training in the path on the basis of this mantra alone. So to underline this contrast to the trainees of inferior faculties, this has been called a "mantra." It is, however, not a mantra in the sense of the four classes of tantra. Although the past Kadam masters have taught visualization of the image of the great mother [perfection of wisdom] and recitation of this mantra, they did not speak of visualizing oneself as the mother perfection of wisdom. Although some Tibetans conduct empowerment ceremonies of this, [they are mistaken for] the basis of practices [namely the perfection of wisdom and tantra] remains different.

Therefore, if one contemplates the meaning of the *profound endowed with the four aspects* and *eight aspects* and, while being mindful of the mode of treading the five paths, and after reciting this mantra if one exclaims the power of its truth and claps their hands, one will receive great waves of blessing. This is just like how, in the past, Indra was able to vanquish the forces of mara as a result of contemplating the meaning of this mantra.

Exhortation to Train by Means
of Summarizing the Subject Matter

The third [the exhortation to train by means of summarizing the subject matter] is presented in the following passage: "Avalokiteshvara, the bodhisattva, the great being. Excellent!..." This is easy to understand.

The statement that not only our teacher but all the tathagatas rejoiced indicates Avalokiteshvara's response and presents the teacher's own enlightened intention.

The Assembly Members' Delight
and Their Pledge to Uphold

The fourth [the assembly members' delight and their pledge to uphold this teaching] is presented in the passage "As the Blessed One uttered these words, the venerable Shariputra...rejoiced and hailed what the Blessed One had said."

Of the three classes of scriptures—those that emerge through being given permissions, those that are inspired, and those that are verbally uttered—the prologue at the beginning and the expression of praise [at the end] are scriptures of permission. The dialogue in the middle is an inspired scripture, while the granting of affirmation to Avalokiteshvara is an uttered scripture.

Furthermore, this sutra is endowed with five perfect factors as well. The prologue presents the four perfect factors—teacher, time, place, and assembly—while up to the end of the queries and responses presents the perfect factor of teaching.

Dedication

Thus I utter:

As the creator of speech who is unexcelled in speech
blessed the throats of beings like Holder of White Lotus[41]
and Shariputra, a discourse such as this has emerged.
How is this possible other than with the teachings of the
    able one?

By hearing it or focusing on it and through this,
even if one gives the letters [of this to others] several times,
it reveals what has been taught. This fortune to uphold
the understanding at will is this very gift of the teacher.

Still, by following in the footsteps of the sublime father,
and by seeking refuge in the meditation deities,
may I continue to enjoy the fortune to partake
in the celebrations of upholding the teachings of the Buddha.[42]

Colophon

This brief exposition of the meaning of the words of the *Heart of Wisdom*, made easy to understand, has been put into writing by the Dharma-speaking monk Jamyang Gawai Lodrö. This has been based on what appears to be the convergent [understanding] of Vimala's extensive commentary, the summary composed by Ngok Lekshe, and the short commentary written by the highly learned

Kamalashila,[43] and also by ensuring that there is no contamination of self fabrications.

　May through the force of uniting the pure aspirations of all those who have been associated with the work of printing this—the scriber Ngawang Chögyal of the Phukhang House of Drepung Loseling [Monastery] and those who have provided material facilities—all sentient beings swiftly attain the four bodies of a buddha.[44]

　Sarvamangalam!

Notes

1 *Buddhist Wisdom: The Diamond Sutra and The Heart Sutra.* Translation and commentary by Edward Conze, preface by Judith Simmer-Brown (New York: Vintage Books, 2001), p. xxiii.

2 For more on the use of the *Heart Sutra* to overcome obstacles, see Donald S. Lopez, Jr., *Elaborations on Emptiness: Uses of the Heart Sūtra* (Princeton NJ: Princeton University Press, 1998).

3 For a more detailed treatment of the twelve links, see His Holiness' commentary in *The Meaning of Life: Buddhist Perspectives on Cause and Effect.* Translated and edited by Jeffrey Hopkins. (Boston: Wisdom Publications, 2000).

4 The six primary afflictions are attachment, anger, pride, ignorance, afflicted views, and afflicted doubt. The twenty derivative afflictions are wrath, vengeance, spite, envy, and malice, which are derived from anger; miserliness, self-satisfaction, and mental excitement, which are derived from attachment; concealment, mental dullness, faithlessness, procrastination, forgetfulness, and inattentiveness, which are derived from ignorance; pretension, dishonesty, lack of shame, inconsideration of others, unconscientiousness, and distraction, which are derived from both attachment and ignorance.

5 Shantideva, *Guide to the Bodhisattva's Way of Life.* See especially chapter 5.

6 *Chatushatakashastrakarika*, 8:15. For an alternative translation of this verse,

see *Yogic Deeds of Bodhisattvas: Gyel-tsap on Aryadeva's Four Hundred* by Geshe Sonam Rinchen (Ithaca: Snow Lion, 1994).

7 The ten unwholesome actions are killing, stealing, sexual misconduct, lying, slandering, harsh speech, idle speech, covetousness, ill will, and holding wrong views.

8 For a brief explanation of this sutra's contextualization of the notion of identitylessness, see the section in chapter 9 entitled, "The Mind-only Interpretation."

9 For more on this topic, see chapter 11.

10 For an authoritative translation of some of these foundational treatises, see *The Middle Length Discourses of the Buddha,* translated by Bhikkhu Ñanamoli and Bhikkhu Bodhi (Boston: Wisdom Publications, 1995).

11 This translation of the *Heart Sutra* is from the Tibetan version, the edition used by H.H. the Dalai Lama for his discourse in Mountain View, California, in 2001. At that teaching a translation by John D. Dunne undertaken at the request of Wisdom Publications was printed in the program booklet. In this volume, however, I have chosen to provide my own translation so that the English version will be more consistent with the Dalai Lama's commentary. In doing so, I have consulted Jamyang Galo's brief commentary (see appendix) for introducing paragraph breaks to the Tibetan text to help with the flow in the English translation. In addition, I have consulted John D. Dunne's translation and also Edward Conze's much earlier English translation, which has held a special place in my heart for a long time.

12 In the Tibetan literary tradition, segment numbers are provided at the beginning of scriptures while the chapter titles are provided at the end. The *Heart Sutra* has only one segment. For comments on the Tibetan custom of dividing scriptures into segments, see pp. 66–67.

13 The eight mundane concerns are actually four polar pairs of concerns.

To be defiled by them means to be motivated in any action by attachment to the first or fear of its opposite: gain and loss, pleasure and pain, renown and infamy, praise and blame.

14 According to Mahayana sutras, there are ten bodhisattva levels, beginning from the first instance when the bodhisattva attains direct insight into emptiness on the path of seeing. The original Sanskrit term *bhumi* literally means the "ground;" these levels are defined in terms of the progressive stages of advancement in the bodhisattva's deepening insight into emptiness.

15 The six perfections (*paramitas*) are the trainings in generosity, ethical discipline, forbearance, joyous effort, concentration, and wisdom.

16 The three basic rites of a monastic community are (1) the bi-monthly confessional ceremonies, (2) the three-month rainy season retreat, and (3) the ending of the rainy season retreat.

17 Historically, the various traditions of Vinaya evolved from the four main divisions of the earliest Buddhist school, called *Vaibhashika*. The Theravada tradition—which today flourishes in countries such as Sri Lanka, Thailand, and Burma—and the *Mulasarvastivada* tradition of Vinaya practice followed by Tibetan Buddhism were two of those four subdivisions of the early Buddhist school. The Vinaya tradition practiced in Chinese Buddhism is that of the *Dharmagupta* School, a subset of one of the four Vaibhashika traditions. Furthermore, the Theravada Vinaya is based on the *Patimokkha Sutta*, the "individual liberation scripture," found in the Pali language, while the Mulasarvastivada Vinaya tradition followed by Tibetan Buddhists is based on the Sanskrit version, the *Pratimoksha Sutra*. The Pali text enumerates 227 precepts for a fully ordained monk, whereas the list in the Sanskrit version is 253. This difference arises from the different way of listing the fifth class of secondary precepts. In the Pali tradition there are 75 on this list, while in the Sanskrit tradition there are 112.

18 Chandrakirti, *Supplement to the Middle Way*, 6:86. For an alternative translation of this verse, see C. W. Huntington, *The Emptiness of Emptiness*
(Honolulu: University of Hawai'i, 1989). The Sanskrit word *tirthikas*
refers here to the proponents of the non-Buddhist ancient Indian
schools.

19 For a more extensive explanation of the relationship between causes
and their effects, see Tsong-kha-pa, *The Great Treatise on the Stages of the Path
to Enlightenment* (Ithaca: Snow Lion, 2000), pp. 209–14.

20 In order to uphold ethical norms of what to adopt and what to avoid,
the Mind-only School developed a complex theory of how our perceptions of the world arise from propensities that exist naturally in us.
Some texts mention as many as fifteen such propensities, but all of them
are included in four primary propensities: (1) for perceiving and believing in an objective reality; (2) for perceiving similarities; (3) for unenlightened existence; and (4) for language. The Mind-only School asserts
that these basic propensities arise from the imprints of our past habit-
ual ways of seeing the world, and they govern our everyday experience.

For instance, when we look at a chair, we sense that "this object is
a chair." This perception embodies our propensity to see similarities.
But not only does the object appear as a chair, it also appears as the
basis of the word "chair." This aspect of the perception manifests our
propensity for language. Both of these aspects of our perception are
valid. However, the third aspect of this perception is that the object is
the referent of the term "chair" in an objective, substantial sense, as if
the chair possessed an independent status. The Mind-only School
argues that this propensity to believe in the objective existence of the
chair is false. We can see from this that a single perceptual experience,
such as looking at a chair, has different aspects, some of which are
valid and some of which are invalid. The Mind-only School says that
the valid aspects can serve as a basis for upholding the Buddha's ethical teachings on what to adopt and what to avoid.

21 On the problems surrounding the identification of the scriptural source of this oft-quoted statement, see my note 15 in H. H. the Dalai Lama, *The World of Tibetan Buddhism* (Boston: Wisdom Publications, 1994), p. 160.

22 This passage of the sutra is frequently cited in Tsongkhapa's writings on the Middle Way view of emptiness.

23 In Vajrayana meditation practice, it is thus emphasized that when one meditates on emptiness within the context of deity yoga, it is important to choose a basis for one's meditation. This basis can be the aspect of the mind that will retain its continuity throughout an individual's lives until the attainment of enlightenment. The fact that the mind will continue on into the stage of enlightenment is one of the main reasons that the mind is often emphasized as the focus of emptiness meditation. This is also the case in other practices such as Mahamudra and Dzogchen, wherein the main focus of meditation on emptiness is one's mind.

24 Nagarjuna, *Fundamentals of the Middle Way*, 24:8. For an alternative translation of this verse, see Frederick J. Streng, *Emptiness: A Study in Religious Meaning* (Nashville: Abingdon Press, 1967), p. 213.

25 Nagarjuna, *Fundamentals of the Middle Way*, 1:1–2.

26 For a detailed list and explanation of these eighteen elements, see H. H. the Dalai Lama, *Opening the Eye of New Awareness* (Boston: Wisdom Publications, 1999), pp. 32–34.

27 Nagarjuna, *Fundamentals of the Middle Way*, 18:5. For an alternative translation, see Frederick J. Streng, *op. cit.*, p. 204.

28 Tsongkhapa, *In Praise of Dependent Origination*, vv. 45–46. For an alternative translation, see *Splendor of an Autumn Moon*, trans. by Gavin Kilty (Boston: Wisdom Publications, 2001), p. 239.

29 Chapter 2 ("Pramanasiddhi"), verse 130b.

30 Shantideva, *Guide to the Bodhisattva's Way of Life*, 8:157. For an alternative translation, see Santideva, *The Bodhicaryavatara* (New York: Oxford University Press, 1996), p. 102.

31 The version of Jamyang Galo's text upon which this translation has been based is a handwritten copy that was printed on stencil in Buxar by Drepung Loseling Monastery. This is also the same version in the PL480 collection of the Library of Congress, USA, where it is listed as No. 90-915034. Certain parts of this edition appear to suffer from corrupt spellings and, in a few cases, possible omissions. I shall identify those that I detect in my notes. However, until we locate a more reliable and preferably an earlier woodblock edition of the text, all my suggestions for correction must remain provisional.

32 In the Tibetan text, this heading appears here as "The assembly members' delight and an advice *(gdams pa)* to uphold." Later in the text where this section actually appears, it is listed as "their pledge *(dam bca' ba)* to uphold." This second spelling suits the author's reading of that particular section of the *Heart Sutra*. So I think that the use of this word "advice" *(gdams pa)* here is either the scribe's error or the author's own oversight.

33 In the Tibetan text, this is followed by a heading, which reads "The third is" *(gsum pa ni)*. This, I think, is an error for what follows in the text is most evidently an elaboration of the summary statement that immediately precedes.

34 This is a paraphrase of the *Heart Sutra's* most well-known passage: "Form is emptiness; emptiness is form. Emptiness is not other than form; form is also not other than emptiness."

35 This text is listed in *Tengyur* as *An Exposition of the Heart of Wisdom Well Explained by Lekpai Sherap on the Basis of Supplication to the Master Dipamkara Shrijnana*, Beijing 5222, Tohoku 3823.

36 The full title of Vimalamitra's commentary is *Extensive Exposition of the Heart of the Perfection of Wisdom in Eight Points*, Beijing 5217, Tohoku 3818.

37 In the Tibetan text, on several occasions, the expression *mnyam gzhag de'i gzigs ngor* (within the perspective of such meditative equipoise) has been mistakenly written as *mnyam gzhag de'i gzugs kyi ngor* (on the surface of the form of the meditative equipoise), which does not appear to make sense.

38 This is probably a reference to the Sakya scholar Rongtön Shakya Gyaltsen (1367–1449). So far I have failed to locate Rongtön's commentary on the *Heart Sutra*.

39 "Non-abiding nirvana" is an epithet for the Buddha's nirvana of full awakening. It is so called because it does not abide in the extremes of both unenlightened, samsaric existence and that of the enlightened, isolated peace of individualistic nirvana.

40 They are (1) the "great mind," which refers to the altruistic mind of the Buddha, (2) the "great overcoming," which refers to the overcoming of grasping at self-existence of persons and phenomena, and (3) the "great realization"—the uncontaminated, omniscient wisdom of the buddhas. They are listed in Maitreya's *Ornament of Clear Realizations* as the "three great objectives" *(ched du bya ba chen po gsum)*.

41 An epithet for the bodhisattva Avalokiteshvara.

42 In the Tibetan text, the last line of this stanza reads *nam yang ngoms pa med pa'i bshes gnyen dag*. This appears to be either corrupted or, if correct, it suggests that there is at least one more subsequent stanza. This is an issue that cannot be resolved until we have access to another edition of the text. In the meantime, to make the sense complete, I have read the last line as *nam yang ngoms pa med pa'i dpal thob shog*.

43 Beijing 5221. The author of the Derge catalogue, Zhuchen Tsultrim Rinchen, lists this text as "said to be authored by Kamalashila."

44 This is probably a note inserted by the scriber, the Drepung monk Ngawang Chögyal, himself. Unfortunately he does not tell us the edition of the text that he was copying this from, information that would have been most helpful for future editors.

Bibliography

Conze, Edward, trans. and comm. *Buddhist Wisdom: The Diamond Sutra and the Heart Sutra.* New York: Vintage Books, 2001.

Gyatso, Tenzin, the Fourteenth Dalai Lama. *The Meaning of Life: Buddhist Perspectives on Cause and Effect.* Trans. and ed. by Jeffrey Hopkins. Boston: Wisdom Publications, 2000.

————. *Opening the Eye of New Awareness.* Trans. and introduced by Donald S. Lopez, Jr. Boston: Wisdom Publications, 1999.

———— *The World of Tibetan Buddhism.* Trans. and ed. by Geshe Thupten Jinpa. Boston: Wisdom Publications, 1994.

Hopkins, Jeffrey. *Meditation on Emptiness.* Boston: Wisdom Publications, 1996.

Huntington Jr., C. W. with Geshe Namgyal Wangchen, *The Emptiness of Emptiness.* Honolulu: University of Hawai'i, 1989.

Jinpa, Thupten. *Self, Reality and Reason in Tibetan Philosophy: Tsongkhapa's Quest for the Middle Way.* London & New York: Routledge Curzon, 2002.

Lopez, Jr., Donald S. *Elaborations on Emptiness: Uses of the Heart Sutra.* Princeton NJ: Princeton University Press, 1998.

Ñanamoli, Bhikkhu and Bhikkhu Bodhi, trans. *The Middle Length Discourses of the Buddha.* Boston: Wisdom Publications, 1995.

Rinchen, Geshe Sonam. *Yogic Deeds of Bodhisattvas: Gyel-tsap on Aryadeva's Four Hundred.* Trans. and edited by Ruth Sonam. Ithaca: Snow Lion, 1994.

Shantideva. *The Bodhicaryavatara.* Trans. with introduction and notes by Kate Crosby and Andrew Skilton. New York: Oxford University Press, 1996.

————. *The Way of the Bodhisattva: A Translation of the Bodhicharyavatara.* Trans. by the Padmakara Translation Committee. Boston: Shambhala, 1997.

Streng Frederick J. *Emptiness: A Study in Religious Meaning.* Nashville: Abingdon Press, 1967.

Tsongkhapa, *The Great Treatise on the Stages of the Path to Enlightenment.* Trans. by the Lamrim Translation Committee. Ithaca: Snow Lion, 2000.

————. *The Splendor of an Autumn Moon: The Devotional Verse of Tsongkhapa.* Trans. and introduced by Gavin Kilty. Boston: Wisdom Publications, 2001.

Index